Globalism and The Nation-State

For
Walter Gordon
who foresaw most of this
long before the rest of us.

This book is based on the five-part 1983 Massey Lecture of the same name, which was broadcast in November as part of CBC Radio's "Ideas" series. Executive Producer: Robert Prowse.

Eric William Kierans, P.C., B.A., LL.D. (Hon.), is a well-known and respected Canadian economist. Born in Montreal in 1914 and educated at Loyola College and McGill University, his career included that of President of the Montreal and Canadian stock exchanges, extensive business experience, as well as the political offices of Minister of Revenue for Quebec, Director of The McGill School of Commerce, Minister of Health for Quebec, President of the Quebec Liberal Federation, candidacy for the Federal leadership (Liberal) in 1968, and federal Cabinet Minister with the positions of Postmaster General and Minister of Communications. After resigning from the Cabinet in 1971, he returned to McGill University as Professor of Economics and continued lecturing, writing, and serving as a consultant and in other senior positions for financial and government institutions across Canada.

Professor Kierans is currently teaching in the Department of Economics, Dalhousie University.

Contents

Foreword

Williamsburg provided, as Professor Abraham Rotstein has pointed out, an excellent metaphor for dealing with concerns that have engaged me since the Honourable Walter Gordon's budget of June 13, 1963—the vulnerability of the Canadian economy and the recognition that our status, in American eyes, was simply that of an economic and political satellite.* While I had vigorously opposed the minister's budget, it became clear to me in December, 1965, when the United States government imposed guidelines on their subsidiaries operating in Canada, that Mr. Gordon had been right to express his anxieties. For the guidelines had involved a principle—the principle that the American government had the right to dictate the investment and reinvestment policies, the purchasing practices, and the financial operations of Canadian companies in which Americans had more than a 10 per

---

*Such concerns also appear in Professor Kierans' resignation from the Federal cabinet; see Appendix C.

cent interest. What price Canadian sovereignty and jurisdiction in such a state of affairs?

Canada was later granted an exemption from these particular directives by a foreign government, but this is beside the point. The brutal fact of Canada's vulnerability to a neighbour's economic and political pressures had been bared for all to see. Henceforth the issue became—"Is Canada sovereign or is it not?"

When David Ricardo formulated his doctrine of comparative advantage, he was writing about trade between sovereign and independent nations, each choosing its own areas of specialization. He was not talking about trade between a motherland and its colonies where the size of the home markets and the direction of investment made the colony a supplier to the needs of the heartland. This was not trade but rather an in-house transfer of resources. In an imperial federation, the colonies and dependencies have no room to pursue the balanced growth of their own economies. Their role is to consolidate and strengthen the empire by undertaking those patterns of development that will converge with the needs and objectives of the empire.

If one wants to create a world economy, one does it in the Soviet manner. One creates a bloc, a collection of nations and peoples ruled over and dominated by a powerful state. The centre is supreme and imperial and all the rest are satellites. Then, and only then, can one speak of a collective world, a world economy in which the factors and resources of all the member nations are integrated in the pursuit of one set of goals, the goals of the governing bloc. The cohesion of the bloc is effective when the goals of the satellites—balanced growth, as an example—are sacrificed to the imperial aims of the bloc itself. Then the supreme power in the heartland can speak of combining the labour of some members, the minerals and petroleum resources of another, with the technology and capital of the centre to produce an optimum output geared to heartland objectives— world domination or whatever. In such an integrated economy, East or West, we can be certain of two results—the subordination of consumer interests in all parts of the bloc (including the dominant centre), and the vulnerability and dependence of the satellite members as their own specialized contributions to bloc production creates imbalance and distortion at home.

Within the Soviet world economy, the nation-state, as an independent political unit free to choose its own principal directions, no longer exists. The argument in 1983 seems to be, at least in the current Washington orthodoxy, that a similar cohesion must be assented to, if not imposed, in the West. The emphasis is tilting from the alliance outlook, all for one and one for all, to the imperial view—all for one and the one *is* all.

Economists who speak of a new world economy are thinking of the world, or the Western part of it, as one vast production line, turning out so many machines or gallons of paint or whatever. It is international production, using "the capital of one nation, the land of another, the labour of a third." The economic region is not a nation but the world itself.

The same people generally think of themselves as the core, the heartland, with all the rest a periphery. American economists, in particular, who describe the concept of international production as a breakthrough replacing classical (Ricardian) trade theory and salute it as a profound insight of great intellectual power forget, or do not know, that the Soviet bloc has been organized in this fashion since the days of the first five-year plan. Canadians, of course, see nothing new in all this, since Great Britain organized her colonies in this fashion and, at least since 1854, the United States has so regarded Canada as its economic appendage.

Extending the Monroe Doctrine to cover Europe and Japan made the commitment to the policies of international production and a supranational allocation of resources seem as natural as the night following the day. The result would be an economy of the Western world via the restoration of the hegemony of the United States. This unified conception of the world is not an economic arrangement of production, consumption, and distribution patterns designed to satisfy the varying needs and objectives of nations in differing circumstances, but rather an arbitrary and ruthless imposition of productive processes geared to securing nuclear supremacy and undisputed world dominance as the first and major objective of a tightly controlled Western bloc.

Efficiency in international (or national) production of anything is easy. Settle on what it is that you want to produce and then produce it. The economic problems do not lie in the production process. They surface later in the exchange process, in the market place, in the consumption and consequent distribution of incomes arising from the particular production if it is consumed. The pattern of production in a market economy is dictated by the adding up of the choices of consumers, which, being infinitely varied, do not admit of less than numberless producing units—from family units and selfless communities willing to work for no reward or very little, the growing informal (bartering-services) economy espoused by the Vanier Institute, to the local, provincial, regional, and national markets that integrate the myriad decisions to exchange and the even greater number of decisions not to exchange.

In a world-command economy, which is not a market economy, the organization of production and consumption obviously lends itself to international production. Nuclear missiles come to mind. But in this instance, production may be divided between a Soviet bloc and a United States bloc. Surely, according to the logic of the one-world economists, the two should then get together and meld their technology, resources, capital, and labour and produce at optimum efficiency, say, fifty thousand nuclear missiles. Since this production is its own consumption, they could each take twenty-five thousand missiles home, to do with as they will, so long as they leave the rest of us with the freedom to look after our own problems of poverty, unemployment, inflation, and pollution of the environment.

To withstand the Soviet might, it is not necessary for the nations of the West to regroup themselves into provinces within a great United States empire and so become the very thing that we despise. Yet there are many in the corridors of power in Washington who bitterly regret the decline in the capacity of the United States to control and direct the course of political and economic change, as it was able to do in the two decades following the Second World War.

The following lectures were recorded prior to the United States intervention in Grenada. The circumstances surrounding the invasion make clear that the United States has little faith or confidence in alliance systems (and even in some allies) and is in fact determined to play a role that emphasizes its power, both military and economic, to control events—and this with or without the consent of members of the alliance.

To have power is to use it. The sources of United States power are the nuclear force, a market well in excess of three trillion dollars, and a veto power over IMF decisions on the granting of loans and credits to nations.

The nuclear umbrella is of incalculable benefit to Europe and important to Japan. Canada would be severely damaged by even a partial closing of the American market to our goods. The less affluent nations, living with the burden of monstrous debts and interest repayments, depend on U.S. good will as they plead their case for further loans. These are strong cards, and, in the game of power politics, there should be little doubt that the United States can and will play them.

The view from Washington holds that the policies of the nation-states of the West *must* conform to the needs of global security as defined by the United States. The use of such terms as "alliances," "participation," and "interdependence" has been abandoned as foolish rhetoric that influences no one. The remaining nation-states of the Western alliance, therefore, face the double challenge of maintaining their own sovereignty and independence in face-to-face confrontation with their dominating partner while, at the same time, making clear to the Soviet bloc that there is in this diversity the real strength that comes from knowing that freedom is worth defending and that it will be defended at all costs.

Twenty-two years ago a director of a large Swiss bank gave me his view of Canada as seen from his boardroom in Geneva. "Your country is all but face-less," he said gently, describing our passivity and inertia in the face of American initiatives.

Later, in the rather long discussion, he mused, "You do have cards of your own to play, if you would only act instead of being always acted upon. After all, if the United States cannot get along with Canada, who can they get along with?"

If we do not want to live in the bipolar world of perpetual confrontation, we, as a people, should say so—loud and clear.

Professor Eric Kierans

Department of Economics,
Dalhousie University,
Halifax, Nova Scotia.

Chapter
One

The Meaning of Williamsburg

The theme of these lectures reflects an anxiety for the continued freedom and independence of the constitutionally-governed nation-states. In 1983, military security demands the close collaboration of the nations of the West, but does it require the formation of a totalitarian bloc to match the satellitic cohesion of the Soviets? Secondly, given the increasing pressure for ever-greater levels of economic integration, how much freedom will nation-states have to set their own objectives and to choose their particular policy instruments and institutions?

Military security in a nuclear age and the alleged efficiency of economic interdependence are the arguments used to force the industrial nations of the West along the road to political unification. At Williamsburg, Virginia, the seven leading industrial nations put their stamp of approval on American defence proposals as well as the U.S. program to promote the convergence of the economic policies and performance of the group.

The meaning of Williamsburg is quite simply that the global community has arrived and that the industrial nations of the West are transforming themselves into a superbloc to match the cohesion and forced unity of the members of the Warsaw Pact. NATO, the OECD, the IMF, and GATT are organizations without authority or the power to make decisions. Making recommendations, searching for consensus, dialogue and debate—the time for all this is past. Government of the Western world, under the hegemony of the United States, is a distinct possibility by 1990.

The summit statement on arms control of May 29, 1983,* agreed to by all seven nations, contained the following declaration: "the security of our countries is indivisible and must be approached on a global basis." President Reagan, in supporting the declaration, effectively extended the protection of the Monroe Doctrine from North, Central, and South America to Europe and Japan. With this single sentence, the industrial nations of the West became a single, homogeneous bloc, and the six members underlined their gratitude for and submission to the absolute dominance of the United States by agreeing to "proceed with the planned deployment of the U.S. systems (Cruise and Pershing II) in Europe at the end of 1983"—unless the Soviet Union agrees to meaningful and constructive concessions in the negotiations on strategic weapons, intermediate-range nuclear missiles, and chemical weapons.

*The complete text is printed in Appendix A.

Confirming the objective "to maintain sufficient military strength to deter any attack, to counter any threat, and to ensure the peace," the conference studied the American proposals for the integration of the national economies and the convergence of economic policies. Military strength depends on productive power, and the optimization of productive power requires the clear recognition of the bloc's priorities, the organization, acquisition, and development of the resources of all the members, and the allocation and budgeting of the total resources for maximum efficiency and output.

Ignoring the desire of each nation to retain as much freedom as possible in setting its own priorities and the policies necessary to the resolution of its particular problems, the conference placed the needs of the bloc itself ahead of the requirements of the merging members. "East-West economic relations should be compatible with our security interests," states the declaration,* thus placing a large question mark on the future of European-Soviet trade, though not necessarily on American grain exports.

The path to economic unification is spelled out in an annex detailing the necessary "near-term policy actions leading to convergence of economic conditions in the medium term."

In the realm of monetary policy, all nations are agreed on a "disciplined non-inflationary growth of monetary aggregates and appropriate interest rates," a clear assumption that the relative position of the members is in equilibrium.

The complete text is printed in Appendix B.

The nations will pursue a deflationary fiscal policy by exercising restraint over government spending, by reducing structural budget deficits, and by keeping in mind the impact of tax and expenditure policies on interest rates and economic growth. Since the seven members are also expected to increase their support of NATO and military expenditures, it is clear that the interests of consumers are being subordinated to the objectives of the military union.

Just as restrictive of national freedom to make one's own choices as the monetary and fiscal packages is the agreement to pursue greater stability of exchange rates and policies of convergence and co-ordinated intervention in exchange markets. This attempt to introduce a 1983 version of the Bretton Woods monetary system is bound to fail for the same reason that Bretton Woods failed. One cannot packet together nations of unequal size, resource wealth, and productive power except under military and economic pressures.

It is sensible to agree that for some purposes, such as military security in this nuclear era, nations must join in collaboration and alliance. It is a question, however, if the creation of a supranational bloc on the same model as the Soviet system is called for. Internalizing all military power in a single high command would be the surrender of the very values and traditions that we cherish, the freedom to choose the principal directions of national life. For military security inevitably demands the integrated economic community, and this adds up to the loss of national autonomy. Countries that have no control over their monetary system, their tax and expenditure policies, and their exchange rates are not sovereign.

Collective action under the leadership of the superior power, the United States, has been the Western option, but it has, until recently, taken the form of alliances and treaty organizations in which all partners are heard and presumably their views taken into account. The motivating principle behind the degree of centralization accepted at Williamsburg seems to be a conscious longing within the American leadership for the same terrifying accumulation of powers and degree of cohesion and political conformity in the West that is the Soviet reality. One has to ask if it is necessary to convert an organized system of alliances into a cabinet of satellites and so degrade the very system of Western traditions of pluralism and liberty that we proclaim, in order to achieve the alleged advantages of the efficiency and discipline that we impute to the members of the Warsaw Pact.

Centralization of power and authority that begins with the military and economic sectors leads inevitably to pressures for the integration of all decision making and a degree of commitment and obedience to the bloc's objectives that leave only marginal room for the national purposes. Such a commitment can hardly be expected of democratic nations possessing a long history of freedom to set their own goals and to choose the instruments of policy necessary to their achievement.

To create a Western bloc involves the location of the foundations of military and economic power in a single authority, the most powerful member being the United States. The foundations are the centralization of all decision making; the unification of the total resource base of the member nations; the control and allocation of all resources, human and material, to achieve maximum output; forced resolution of conflicts between the bloc's objectives and national goals; and finally the subordination of the interests of consumers and the standard of living generally to the goals of increased productive power and military security. Efforts to regiment the Western world in this fashion would require, if not the terrorization practised in the East, enormous economic pressure and the terrifying threat to abandon the recalcitrant to the nuclear nightmare.

Before we proceed further in the substitution of the present system of international relations, the pluralism of the Western alliances, for the tightly knit bloc control that typifies the Soviet monolith, we should examine very carefully the pressures that are being exerted. One virtue of the present international system is that, while the United States is clearly the leader of the West, it has to take account of and bring into consensus or compromise the views of its partners. The creation of an American-Japanese-European superbloc under American hegemony allows no such flexibility or dialogue. We become more and more the satellites, forced to subordinate national priorities for the interests of the bloc system.

If we go this route, we have to ask ourselves how different would the two systems of political control over the lives and times of our citizens then be. The major difference would appear to be the greater diffusion of property and private power in the West, but how quickly could that be eroded in the new system of centralized decision making?

Given a superbloc in the West, the two political systems would have much more in common than is supposed. Each could annihilate the other with its nuclear power. Each would emphasize the growth of industrial and productive power as a priority. Each would subordinate the interests of the consumer to military and economic growth objectives. As the people of the Soviet bloc are powerless before the bureaucratic authority, so too would the people of the West lose power to our corporate and public monuments of stone. The difference would be one of degree.

The argument for military globalism is that only then would the West have the cohesion, discipline, and the nuclear inventory and configuration that could effectively oppose the Russian menace. Experts, however, such as Admiral Robert Falls of Canada, Rear Admiral LaRocque of the United States, and Field Marshal Lord Carver of the United Kingdom, tell us that we have more than enough nuclear weaponry already in position to inflict untold casualties and destruction on the Soviet Union. Since the enemy can do the same to us, both sides are in the same position— no possible victory, only complete and utter defeat.

It is a good thing to know that the Western alliance has more than enough nuclear missiles; the bad thing is that we keep on building more; the worst thing of all is not to know why—why more production, why more deployment, why a superbloc of the West. If we are not satisfied with the power to annihilate, what will we be satisfied with?

NATO officials have themselves maintained that the 1979 decision to station intermediate-range nuclear missiles in Europe was psychological and political rather than military. The NATO generals, in their venture into psychology, argue that the highly visible death-dealing Cruise and Pershing II missiles deployed on European soil will comfort the populations of Europe. It is at least arguable that fear, despair, and hysteria at the sight of some 572 of these monsters of destruction may be the paramount response, with Europe facing a hot and riotous period as installations go forward.

NATO and the Warsaw Pact are the instruments of their respective masters. They are neither political nor executive in respect of their powers. Both NATO and the Warsaw Pact are genuine deterrents against perceived threats. We have here the classic instance of two bureaucracies leaning upon each other for nourishment. As each screams its defiance, they guarantee the continuity and growth of the functions and purposes of the other. Russia uses the belligerence of NATO to maintain its grip over its Eastern satellites, while the Warsaw Pact serves as the rationale for stripping the industrial nations of the West of sovereignty in their military and economic policies and creating the United States supranational bloc.

The summit conference is now an established coming together with the purpose of stopping the Russian threat. With this objective there can be no dispute. In a nuclear era, we can hardly find security on a nation-by-nation defence. The meaning of Williamsburg, however, is that we intend to create the identical military and economic monolith in the West that exists in the East. Thus there will be two, and two only, supranational powers facing each other, each power believing that the other is all black while absolute right and justice remains with it alone. Williamsburg brings not a movement toward the foundation of a true international order but the absolute polarization of two political crusades treading a head-on collision course.

Williamsburg has brought us back to the bipolar world of the 1950s and John Foster Dulles, with Moscow speaking for the East and Washington speaking for the Canadians, Europeans, and Japanese. In the fluid, unpredictable, nuclear atmosphere of violence, the polarization can only deepen the tensions and expand the areas of conflict, making reassessment and negotiation all the more difficult since neither side will want to risk the possible humiliation of retreat and loss of face.

Williamsburg reaffirmed the deployment of the intermediate-range nuclear missiles in Europe; it announced the creation of a Japanese-American-European superbloc. We already live in a world that faces annihilation in the event of a nuclear war. Our future will be, as Jonathan Schell describes, "the republic of insects and grass." The superbloc set forth at Williamsburg adds little if anything to the military unification that already exists at NATO. It makes little sense to add to the arms or improve the system when you have already passed well beyond the point of mutual annihilation. If more arms are redundant, more food, water, education, health, and housing for the underprivileged of this world are not. Reducing the production of arms by two weeks would enable us to double our spending on these vital elements in the world's standard of living.

Despite all the headlines, all the editorials, all the meet-the-press and week-in-review commentaries, there is no evidence that the danger of nuclear war is growing. There can be no winners in a nuclear holocaust. There is something fundamentally irrational in the confrontation of two powers that keep their citizens in anxious suspense even though each has brought the other to a standstill. When victory is not possible, when further action means utter defeat, it is time to accept the deadlock, relieve the tensions, and create the environment that will enable all peoples to pursue the ways and means to creative living.

An American-Japanese-European economic bloc to support the military stance makes good sense from the American point of view, if it can be obtained under the terms outlined in the Williamsburg agreement, which in effect defined the basic economic unit as the Western world. Given the total commitment of the United States to guaranteeing the security of the industrial West, including Japan, the fusion of economic policies as they converge with American objectives follows as the necessary condition.

Thus President Reagan outlined the agreement as "policy actions leading to convergence of economic conditions in the medium term." Essential to the agreement is the understanding that East-West economic relations should hinge upon and be compatible with the security interests of the West. This restores the United States to the unquestioned political, economic, and military dominance that it enjoyed in the two decades prior to its involvement in Vietnam.

That the United States should be the heartland, the core, of Western values and principles is not in dispute. That it should exercise leadership, persuasion, and direction by example is again not the issue. That the

United States should be in a position to impose and to dictate policies and priorities for the other nations of the West would be the end of the politics and pluralism of the Western world. It is this that is unacceptable.

Williamsburg not only defined the industrial West as a global community, it outlined some of the terms of global governance. The leaders agreed to maintain appropriate interest rates and to avoid the inflationary growth of monetary aggregates. They further agreed to reduce their budget deficits by exercising stringent control over government expenditures—at least in the areas of housing, education, health and welfare, and social security, but presumably not in the area of military and defence expenditures, where all members are expected to increase their shares of spending. Equally fundamental is the agreement to work for stabilized exchange markets and, by restricting the use of exchange-rate policy to solve critical national problems, so to strip away the flexibility open to sovereign and autonomous nations and their elected leaders. In other words, the needs of the bloc take precedence over the particular priorities of the member nations.

The problem with extending the concept of interdependence from the military to the economic sector is that we are dealing with the creation of a bloc composed of nations which are now sovereign, which vary in resource wealth, size of markets, needs for capital, and are unequal in productivity and overhead costs. The policies of convergence leave no room to manoeuvre for the solution to these imbalances and the problems that they bring.

The heightened anxiety caused by the increasing polarizations of the two superpowers prevents people from arguing the unsupported and unproven claims that economic interdependence will yield a greater output and that maintaining the benefits of their greater efficiency is vital to Western survival. The blunt facts are that economic interdependence demands the integration of national economies and, therefore, the denial of freedom to an elected government to address a nation's problems and priorities.

A nation will then be defined quite simply as an area, the part of a greater entity, an area where resources are plentiful or an area where labour is cheap or an area where capital is plentiful. In the relevant market of the West, some regions will specialize in steel production, others in chemicals, pulp and paper, cars, agricultural products, etc. Engineers, using technical principles of location theory, will put populations, money, and land in their computers and position the producing facility accordingly. Unstated is the basic assumption that, to make economic interdependence work, there must be a perfect mobility of labour—that is, people must be willing to follow capital, the more perfectly mobile factor, as it moves across nations and continents. Equally unstated and undebated is the pretence that immigration laws and other restrictions do not exist.

The free movement of goods, services, capital, and persons across borders—"what an arrogant and pretentious statement." And what a peculiar definition of freedom when the price of a job requires workers to leave home, heritage, culture, tradition, language, and the community of friends and family.

Globalism is defined in economic terms as the optimal allocation (use) of men and women, resources and capital, across the broad spectrum of the bloc. Globalism, therefore, is specialization—but specialization means an ever-growing dependency. Nations become famous for making the wings of a plane but not the fuselage, for mining the ore but not milling it, for cutting down the trees but importing the furniture. Gone is the balanced growth that would enable a state to offer the wide range of career opportunities to a youth educated at great expense.

The specialization process imposes a planned dependency on a nation. Specialization makes interdependence necessary after it has first made the nation vulnerable by creating an unbalanced economy at home. Specialization in resource exploitation makes the nation subject to the terms and conditions imposed by the industrial powers for its manufacturing needs. The converse is also true.

Consider the logic of international economic interdependence, that is, the deployment of the resources of the globe according to a single most efficient scheduling, an abstract idea at best. Putting the mental image to work, planners then talk glowingly of a gross world production that is greater than the sum of the national outputs. Therefore, there are benefits for everyone that remain to be divided, although this is never spelled out.

If we accept the assumption—which, incidentally, has never been demonstrated—that there will be a greater world output, how is it to be shared? Who will decide the distribution? What percentage will go to improving the standard of living of consumers? What percentage will be invested to increase the military power of the bloc or to validate the perennial promise of a better tomorrow? Will the developed or less developed nations fare best? Which nations will benefit now and which in a distant future?

More fundamentally, who in our brave, new global world will make the decisions? Since each nation's resources have been placed in an international pot and its manpower assigned some partial and specialized role, the nation's freedom to create the instruments necessary to the achievement of its own priorities has been sharply reduced. As the scope for national decision making declines, the instructions coming from the supranational authority increases. The professionals in the international bureaucracies will save the nations of the world from politicians and democratic politics with "all those noisy and incoherent promises, the impossible demands, the hotchpotch of unfounded ideas and impractical plans. . . ."

The new reality with which Canadians must deal is simply this—the United States considers the security of the Western world to be indivisible with its own. Given this purpose and its acceptance by the leading industrial nations, the United States government believes that the task it has undertaken requires that it obtain the unqualified support of the Canadians, the Europeans, and the Japanese in all things political, economic, and military. This is the commitment that was demanded at Williamsburg. This is the commitment that was given.

Williamsburg created the superbloc of the West. Is that superbloc to be America and the six satellites or America and the six allies? In any event, Canada's interests are being poorly served by maintaining the pretence that we are a leading industrial power. We are not. We will never develop the set of strong domestic policies needed to give us control over the directions of our economy until we accept that fact.

Neither Japan nor Europe nor the United States has any intention of helping Canada to become an industrial power. These three industrial giants are each fully capable of supplying a whole range of manufactured products, cars, televisions, steel, radios, capital equipment, tools, and so on, to world markets. Canada's manufacturing potential is neither needed nor will it be welcomed in a world that is moving, despite all protestations, toward increasing protectionism. As these three powers divide the world into industrial spheres of influence, Canada's role will be the supplier of raw materials and energy resources.

Canadian economic policy has, since Confederation, rested on the twin pillars of resource exploitation and capital imports in the colonial form of direct investment. Both policies have been used to such excess that Canada is presently the most vulnerable nation in the world, with its abnormal dependence on export markets, trade cycles, and corporate-capital flows.

To bury ourselves in the bosom of the American superstate is to condemn Canadians forever to the role of suppliers of raw materials. The current trade conflicts between our two countries are an example of the challenge that we face. The United States has always insisted on at least an equilibrium in their balance of trade with us. As we continue to ship billions of dollars of petroleum and mineral resources, they will insist on an equivalent return flow in manufactured goods. For every million dollars in wages and salaries that we export, we will be importing three to four million dollars in American or Japanese or European wages and salaries. In employment terms, we import the labour and effort of three to four workers for every Canadian employed.

How are we as a nation to counteract age-old policies? Are we nasty nationalists if we try? Moving Canadian economic policies into line with those of the United States—consequences, as President Reagan phrased it at Williamsburg—means that we are serving the interests of the bloc rather than our own. It means that Canada will continue to concentrate on the extractive export industries and that domestic and imported capital will abandon the pursuit of industrialization. No industrial policy for Canada but rather the age-old specialization in primary production, with this difference—that it will no longer be the result of market forces and inept government leadership but will be the outcome of the political pressures imposed on us by our trading partners at Williamsburg.

There is no abstract set of international policies that can simultaneously satisfy the needs and requirements of nations as unequal in wealth and power as Canada and the United States. Each nation in the world must define and pursue the strong domestic policies tailored to the development of its own material and human resources. Free trade was the appropriate policy for Great Britain at the zenith of her power in the nineteenth century, but, as Bismarck remarked, "free trade is the policy of the strong," suitable for the nations that were industrial leaders but not necessarily for nations that wanted to be.

Canada's tariff policy of 1879 was a national policy, although it turned out to be counterproductive.

Infant industry protectionism can be made to work if it is accompanied by strong industry creation, as the policies of both the United States and Germany have shown. But Canada failed to create the industries that the tariff was designed to protect, and so the foreign investment and the branch plants took over.

Reaganomics, the emphasis on military power and economic hegemony, is clearly a new national policy designed to establish in the West the measure of cohesion and unification that has existed in the Soviet bloc. Those searching for Canadian policy options in the eighties are not nasty nationalists (what nation blindly places the interests of others before its own?), but Canadians genuinely concerned with the vulnerability of the economy that they are turning over to the next generation.

President Reagan was elected on the promise to make the United States strong again, to restore American prestige and power to the level of the 1950s and the 1960s. He has done so. At Williamsburg, with U.S. nuclear might as the lever, he guaranteed the security of the West on condition that they follow American economic initiatives, and then—less tactfully—become American satellites. A weak and uncompetitive American economy is back in the saddle again, dictating objectives, formulating policies, and assigning roles to the leading nations of the West.

Hyping the unthinkable, the threat of nuclear holocaust, has brought great dividends to the rhetorician of the White House. He cannot lose. When the nuclear tensions lessen, as indeed that insanity must, the United States will have regained undisputed economic leadership of the West, and this is what the exercise is all about.

If Williamsburg is to be Canada's future, that future is bleak indeed.

Chapter
Two

Should There Be a Nation-State?

Wallace Stevens, an American poet, wrote "Anecdote of Men by the Thousand," in which he speaks of the influence that the land has on people.

> *The soul, he said, is composed*
> *of the external world.*
> *There are men of the East, he said,*
> *Who are the East.*
> *There are men of a province*
> *Who are that province*
> *There are men of a valley*
> *Who are that valley. . . .*

The roots of a community are two—the land and the people who come to it. A society is born when a sufficient number of people gather together in a particular place. Each person will have his own reasons for settling in a region—the escape from poverty and oppression, the attraction of a greater freedom and liberty, the hope and promise of greater opportunity.

In time, the people of the region will develop their own ethos, the spirit and dispositions that will provide the set of norms and moral postulates that will govern their economic affairs and their political relations. A community, above all else, expresses the tone, the outlook, the vital force and spirit underlying the living reality of people at work and leisure.

To a great degree nature itself defines and imposes the scope and range if not the limits of opportunities open to the people. It is certain that over the generations there will be in the community a gradual harmonization of values, of expectations, of viewpoints, and of purposes. Thus defined, the community has no problem with its identity.

The external world, as Wallace Stevens writes, affects us, forms us, and commands our work. The challenges facing the east-coast fisherman are not the causes of concern to the prairie farmer or even to the west-coast fisherman. Nor will the responses be the same.

Each accepts his environment for what it is and strives to shape it and to use it rationally and consistently within the limits that nature itself imposes. In this unity of man and environment there is the comtinuity that will survive even the greatest social upheavals. A better example of survival can scarcely be found than the preservation of French Canadian identity and nationalism after military defeat and political catastrophe. As Canon Groulx has written, "La même entité humaine continue sa vie, sur la même terre, dans le même environnement géographique." The strength of the Quebec culture lies in the historical fact that the spiritual beliefs, the outlook, the language, the social institutions, and the political forms remain rooted in the same soil that shaped past generations. And this is true of all communities.

A community, established in its particular living space, soon develops the principles and norms of conduct, the laws and form of government that reflect the beliefs and value systems of its people and guide both internal conduct and a collective approach to the outside world. Local government is a necessity for the members of a community who wish to attain the good of order and the possibility of the collective definition of goals and purpose. Fundamental to this creation of meaningful civic relations is the individual's surrender of his own use of force and the assignment of monopoly powers of coercion to the civil authorities. Without this transfer there could not be community. There would be confusion and anarchy.

Out of the creation of local government by people in particular places flows the range and nature of the specific choices to be made and the goals to be pursued—the third element of the complete society. At the level of community, the horizons embrace all modes of man's existence: the religious, the economic, the social, the scientific, and the cultural. And it is principally at this level, while all the principal directions of living and intending are still open to them, that men and women have the greatest freedom of choice. I take the community to be the solid core of the social system.

What does society lose when successively higher forms of political integration, inspired by unproved and doubtful claims of commercial and financial efficiency, are introduced?

Community economics is an uncomplicated but

rational system. The logic of the community requires that the power to produce be matched with an equivalent capacity to consume. The community priority is a standard of living.

David Riesman's question, "Abundance for what?" is not a relevant question at the community level, where "sharing" is the distinguishing feature and no one need feel alone. If the question were raised, the answer would be clear and unequivocal—a large production and a fair distribution of that production go hand in hand. The circle of economic activity is complete.

Economics was born in the minds of men who lived in a world of court privilege, mercantilism, monopolies, national objectives of empire and trade surpluses, and hated what they saw. "No man produces for the sake of producing and nothing further," said James Mill. "Things are distributed as also exchanged to some end. That end is consumption." As for Adam Smith, "Consumption is the sole end and purpose of all production." And that was that.

As we move to more complex and larger social groupings, Riesman's question raises troubling issues. Production is not necessarily for a good distribution but for more production. Future growth and wealth itself become goals that insert themselves ahead of equitable distribution and improvements in sharing and the present standard of living. Here we are on sensitive ground! John Stuart Mill, writing of the growing abundance provided by the American economy, continued as follows: "and all that these advantages seem to have done for them is that the life of the whole of one sex is devoted to dollar-hunting and of the other to breeding dollar-hunters." This brutal passage, which appeared in the first (1848) edition of Mill's *Principles of Political Economy*, was deleted from the following editions. It is dangerous to suggest that investment in a better tomorrow may leave the living generation hooked on money and nothing else.

Repeating our definition, a community is a sufficient number of people in a particular corner of the world who form a government empowered to define and enforce rules of conduct so that man may know and be free to choose among the principal directions and modes of his existence. In short, the community has no problem with its identity, is the first expression of social humanism and freedom, and is the mould that shapes character, choices, and careers.

The problem of Canadian unity, for example, is to find a way in which the primary importance and fundamental values of community can be maintained in the face of escalating concentration and regimentation at both the political and economic levels. I do not see how this can be accomplished unless our political leaders start from the beginning with the objectives of strengthening our communities and reinforcing our provinces. This will be no simple task in an age of technological, industrial, and financial integration. What the computer imposes upon us is a social discipline, conformity, and homogeneity unknown in all previous history, for corporate and public bureaucracies, if their aims are to be achieved, must define and program the individual in functional terms—man becomes a means to an end, not an end in himself.

This raises the problem of the survival of the individual in a growing bureaucratic society. If power is centralized, the individual loses the protection and security of his community, those who know him and those whom he knows. He is isolated and vulnerable, and the community that once provided the base from which he could develop and make a contribution itself declines in authority and the capacity to support him.

Mill had hoped for the day when "minds ceased to be engrossed by the art of getting on." He wrote that in a stationary state "There would be as much scope as ever for all kinds of mental culture, and moral and social progress; as much room for improving the Art of Living, and much more likelihood of its being improved." His philosophy and sociology were correct, at least in my view, but few economists agreed with him. The historical context, the height of the Industrial Revolution, was not sympathetic.

Similarly, those who speak out against centralization and concentration of power, political or economic, feel instinctively that they are whistling against the wind. Centralization, however, is not a new evil. As Sir Halford Mackinder, famed British geographer, reminded critics of his balanced-economy concept: "You tell me that centralization is the 'tendency' of the age: I reply to you that it is the blind tendency of every age—was it not said nineteen hundred years ago that 'to him that hath shall be given'?"

Centralization, concentration, the accumulation of power and property may well be the tendencies of the age, but they may also be blind tendencies wherein communities are ignored and individuals lose their identity. The governed no longer know their governors.

Nationalist- or provincial-rights movements do not begin with power-mad politicians bent on Balkanizing or "Iranizing" a country. They arise out of dispositions and sentiments that already exist, most often among young people anxious to live a life of challenge and achievement at home. They know that the world moves on, that communities form regional groups which grow into provinces, and the provinces unite to form the federal state. The anxiety centres on the costs of regionalism, nationhood, and now globalism. How much control over their lives and freedom is lost along the way? The land may be strong, but if this foundation of economic independence and personal freedom is owned abroad, what remains of effective, political freedom and the community's capacity to solve problems and to satisfy needs? It is through politics that the spirit of the times is captured, reflected in the polling booths, but then ignored by the elected and the servants of the state.

If I were a political leader, I would find it increasingly difficult to accept the doctrine that Canada, with its distinct economic regions and cultures, should be a strong, centralized country—a heartland centred on Ottawa, Montreal, and Toronto and with all the rest a periphery. In effect, I would be telling the best young people of my province, the educated and the intelligent, to go away. There is no room for you at home.

To make provinces and communities more important is to insist that they strive for more balance in their economies. An economic heartland, the metropolitan centre of colonial days, organizes an economy from the core outward and assigns specialized roles to the outlying regions, which lose their balance and sovereignty and become dependent, lopsided, and vulnerable to change. If you wreck the economic balance of a community or region, can social frustration, cultural poverty, and political ineptness be far behind?

If the roots of a community are its people and its land, then the primary factors of production must also be the people and the land. Capital, then, is a secondary affair derived from the surpluses arising from the utilization of land and labour. Capital is not an original factor of production, however useful and necessary it may be in accelerating the pace of growth and development.

Growth begins with the land and the services of people. If the land is attractive and the yields are good, many will come and stay. If the yields are retained, the community will grow and prosper. If, however, the surpluses are drained away, the community will stagnate and decline in an increasing dependence.

Land and labour are indispensably bound together as the basis of society. Isolating land and forming markets out of it is as great a crime against community as slavery is against humanity. Land is not a product for sale but part of a life-support system which, with labour, precedes the market economy just as it exists prior to the formation of the institutions, laws, and norms of the society. From the point of view of the community, the land and resources must be considered as inalienable, one of the reasons for coming and one of the reasons for staying, the root of sovereignty and the foundation of policies which determine future directions as well as current standards of living.

When we debate the question "should the nation-state survive," the discussion centres around growth, efficiency, the benefits of an international assignment of the factors of production; that discussion is carried on in chambers of commerce, at conferences of economists and bureaucrats both public and private. We seem to forget that economics has to take into account social attitudes, the quality of politics, traditions, language, and human endowments. Above everything else the participation should include people under thirty who will be the more affected than aging corporate executives.

The young are also the ones most likely to have something new to say for, as Keynes remarked, "in the field of economic and political philosophy there are not many who are influenced by new theories after they are twenty-five or thirty years of age, so that the ideas which civil servants and politicians and even agitators apply to current events are not likely to be the newest."

A half-century ago, Berle and Means wrote in their seminal book *The Modern Corporation and Private Property:*

> The rise of the modern corporation has brought a concentration of economic power which can compete on equal terms with the modern state . . . where its own interests are concerned, it even attempts to dominate the state. . . . The law of corporations, accordingly, might well be considered as a potential constitutional law for the new economic state, while business practice is increasingly assuming the aspect of economic statesmanship. . . .

In 1975, discussing the power of large corporate groups and their control of markets, Prime Minister Trudeau was an eloquent witness to the truth of the Berle and Means prophecies—"People are wondering who is in charge of the economy, who's in charge of the society, and they're concerned, they're worried. And they have cause to be."

In a similar vein, President Eisenhower, in his farewell address to the nation, "Liberty Is at Stake," had warned of the dangers to the very structure of American society in the growth of "the total influence—economic, political, even spiritual—" inherent in the size of the military and industrial corporate establishments.

> In the councils of Government, we must guard against the acquisition of unwarranted influence, whether sought or unsought, by the military industrial complex. The potential for the disastrous rise of misplaced power exists and will persist. We must never let the weight of this combination endanger our liberties or our democratic processes. We should take nothing for granted.

Size of firm, economies of scale, efficiencies of concentration, multinational corporations, all are justified by the more productive possibilities assumed to exist in global markets. This conception of the *economic* unification of the world has been justified by George W. Ball, former undersecretary of state in the Kennedy administration, in the following terms:

> In order to survive, man must use the world's resources in the most efficient manner. This can be achieved only when all the factors necessary for the production and use of goods—capital, labor, raw materials, plant facilities and distribution are freely mobilized and deployed according to the most efficient pattern. And this in turn will be possible only when national boundaries no longer play a critical role in defining economic horizons.

And again in the same article:

> Conflict will increase between the world corporation, which is a modern concept evolved to meet the requirements of the modern age, and the nation-state, which is still rooted in archaic concepts unsympathetic to the needs of our modern world.

So there we have it—the modern era has witnessed the progress of civilization from feudal manor to nation-state. It is now, in 1983, time to move on to the emergent world economy, i.e., a unified commercial and corporate view of the world, the organization of production on an international scale.

Economics has as its object the most efficient use of resources at the disposal of a decision-making unit, whether that unit is Aristotle's household, the classical firm, or the corporation or the nation-state. When the world itself is taken as the basic economic unit, the assumption must be that the world is a great anonymous pool of resources both human and physical, yielding goods and services in accordance with their most efficient allocation and without regard to nation-states concerned with their own problems, priorities, and even prejudices. That is the death of the nation-state.

The "archaic" concepts of which Ball speaks are only as "archaic" as the last century. The difference between the 1983 theory of international production and the nineteenth-century theory of international trade is the profound respect that classical economists held for people and for community. A political philosophy is embedded in classical trade theory, for our predecessors were not merely economists but were possessed of a political philosophy as well. Men and women were citizens, the foundation and source of national strength, custodians of the traditions, beliefs, language, laws, and customs of the nation. They were the substance of the state, not mere instruments and factors of production to be transferred to foreign lands at the dictate of capital flows and feedback systems.

No one knew better than David Ricardo the extent of capital exports and emigration from England, but this was not the national purpose. He wrote approvingly of the "natural disinclination which every man has to quit the country of his birth and connexions, and intrust himself with all habits fixed, to a strange government and new laws . . ." The theory of free trade, so suitable for that period of England's hegemony, was designed to build financial power, employment, and industrial strength at home.

In a similar vein, Germany under the influence of the doctrines of Friedrich List and Chancellor Bismarck adopted the opposite policy of protectionism in intense efforts to keep her manpower from emigrating by providing employment at home. Limiting imports to materials containing little labour and few skills, and promoting exports with high wage content soon provided the employment that caused net emigration from Germany to disappear.

Trade in goods, unlike trade in persons, adds to the level of real income in a nation, which leads in turn to an increase in the standard of living and wealth. Nations gained from trading the goods and services in the production of which they had a natural or comparative advantage. They did not gain from draining each other. It would not have occurred to Ricardo, for example, when he spoke of trading English bolts of cloth for Portuguese pipes of wine, that England would be even better off if English capital bought out the vineyards of Portugal and managed their production. Such actions would have invaded a neighbour's sovereignty and reduced its economic independence and, in the long run, was bound to be counterproductive. Such, at least, was the nineteenth-century view. Sovereignty depended not only on a strong citizenry proud of their rights, it also depended on the control of all one's resources. Unlike our political leaders and the current network of civil servants and economic advisers, classical economists believed that the citizenship of those who owned and controlled the land and its natural resources was fundamental to a strong society. A state that is not the master of its own environment can hardly aspire to great status and importance in the assembly of nations. Classical economists incorporated into their principles the society's institutions (private property), national aspirations and objectives, human motivations, drives, and needs, and looked upon the national economy as an ongoing process.

In 1983 the logicians of the world enterprises refuse to recognize that nations are autonomous entities. The world is one, a global system in which each area interacts with the others, and behaviour in any region has repercussions throughout the world economy. Those who refuse to accept the new model of ordering economic activity are labelled nationalists, xenophobes, parochial monopolists, socialists, protectionists, and anti-American.

No one, to my knowledge, of those concerned with the problems of retaining independence in decision making and control over their own choices and value systems has ever held that anyone or any nation can exist apart, or that there would be great value in such isolation if it did exist. Progress is only possible through interaction and interdependence; the diversification that exists between communities adds to the vitality and quality of each.

This acceptance of the worth of other cultures, outlooks, value systems, and social structures leads to an interdependence that is profitable in more than the material sense. Something new is added to one's culture which conserves as it broadens and is subtly changed. There is no dependence in this effect, for nothing is imposed. As Bernard Lonergan has written, "If one is to communicate with persons of another culture, one must use the resources of their culture. To use simply the resources of one's own culture is not to communicate with the other but to remain locked up in one's own." There is no one culture, as anyone from Quebec understands full well; just as there are differences within Canada, so we are entitled to believe in and support a Canada that has a set and shape of values that is distinct from other systems and nations. This does not mean that we would refuse, in the name of independence, to subscribe to a set of moral principles that would serve as the basis for international relations and international law, but it does mean that we contribute what we can of our own values without surrendering our sovereignty, objectives, and policies.

Internationalism can be carried too far, as Keynes pointed out. International trade can become economic warfare as nations attempt to export their unemployment by subsidizing the exports of goods and services on unwilling friends and neighbours. "But if nations can learn to provide themselves with full employment by their domestic policy . . . , there need be no important economic forces calculated to set the interest of one country against that of its neighbours. There would still be room for the international division of labour and for international lending in appropriate conditions." The international community is something added after a national order has been achieved and a society organizes its activities to bring all its citizens a satisfactory standard of living. A nation is entitled to defend itself and its citizens against the power drives of those nations that are willing to risk class warfare at home in order to finance the exports and investments that will secure balance-of-payment surpluses and commercial supremacy. The instability of such competition and economic conflict would effectively block all hopes of achieving a higher unity standing above but rooted in the sovereignty of individual nations. International rules of conduct arise from a proper respect for the particular genius and character of one's neighbours and are defeated by the unrestrained pursuit of one's own interests.

The idea of the world economy is based on the assumption that there exists a one, true, efficient allocation of all the world's human and material resources. This purely mechanistic vision of efficiency, unproved and undemonstrable, cannot accept the intervention of the nation-state with its own ideas of how output and distribution should be pursued. More fundamentally, globalism cannot tolerate politics, the system by which people express their preferences and determine their priorities as a community.

Economic globalism will create a heartland and a heartland creates peripheries, the vulnerable outposts which no level of regional development assistance can reverse. The centre and the heart of the unification zone become strong and affluent as the outlying regions and countries decline in importance and in the capacity to control their own directions. The drain of material resources and skills accelerates, the flow to the core broadens and deepens.

The trouble with the superbloc thesis and the dream world of global efficiency is that it is neither a political nor an economic concept. It is planning, regimentation, bureaucracy. It eliminates initiative, incentive, and the famed freedom of opportunity for new men. One is reminded of Mussolini's grandiose vision of "the complete organic and totalitarian regulation of production with a view to the expansion of the wealth and political power of the Italian people." Williamsburg goes further. It envisions the convergence of policy, planning, and production not for Italy alone but for Italy and the six other leading industrial nations in the proposed Western bloc.

When power is accumulated at the centre, nations are not through, as Professor Kindelberger suggests—they become merely economic units. They are through as political units. The societies become pure economies, the quantitative and mechanical domains of technical coefficients, the inputs and outputs, a world which becomes a great pool of goods and services where the services of labour are separated from the will or needs of the labourer, the services of land and resources from national goals, and the services of capital from the motivations, ambitions, and desires of the proprietor.

Once political power is accumulated in a heartland, is it reasonable to expect that power will then be redistributed back again? Each nation has its own particular set of resources to deal with problems of inflation, unemployment, and poverty. Each nation must maintain its freedom and power to deal directly with them. It cannot be satisfied to wait the day when those who have the power have achieved their objectives nor can it expect that an affluent core will ever willingly decentralize.

Stagnation and inflation, unemployment and poverty are problems that must be faced at the level of the nation-state. The political power to combine and direct its resources, to define the priorities, must remain with the state.

There is a great and immediate urgency for growth and development everywhere. For this to be distributed fairly among all regions of the world, each nation-state must be able to do this job itself. Aid, capital, and technical assistance can be provided by others in supporting but not controlling roles.

Few can believe in a single, global, best allocation of inert and passive factors of production to achieve a purely material growth. Even fewer can expect that a nation can be self-sufficient in so complex and interrelated a world.

Canadians will agree to alliances and arrangements that will add to the strength and security of the Western world, but they will at the same time insist on maintaining the political power and economic freedom to manage their own affairs. Canada must not become a periphery in a superbloc, a supplier of resources to a global centre. Centralization, whatever the advantages—and I see none—drains nations, checks their development, and thwarts their efforts to build the balanced economy that alone can provide sufficient scope and opportunity to our people.

Canada, by insisting on the distinction between the adaptations that are necessary to the security of the West and the pressures that serve simply to centralize power, will be a better ally by remaining an independent nation-state.

Chapter
Three

Is Canada
a Nation-State?

During her 1983 visit to Canada, Prime Minister Thatcher of Great Britain sharply reminded Canadians that they were members of NATO and had agreed at the summit meetings at Williamsburg in May of that year to support NATO policy and particularly the deployment of the Cruise and Pershing II missiles in Europe. It followed that we had no choice but to agree to the testing of the Cruise on Canadian territory; the visiting prime minister implied that that was little enough.

In fact, we agreed to a great deal more than the complete integration of Canadian defence policy with that of the United States, including the latter's stance in the negotiations on arms control with the Soviet Union. We also agreed to make our trade relations with the East compatible with the security interests of the West as defined at Williamsburg. The definitions of compatible economic relations remain to be spelled out.

In the economic field we agreed to align our policies with those of the United States to promote an integration of economic performance in the two economies, as well as with the other leading industrial powers. This alignment included the acceptance of the American lead in restraining the growth of money and credit and in maintaining appropriate interest rates. We further agreed to reduce budget deficits by curtailing government expenditures in areas other than defence, since this would not be compatible with our NATO obligations and, since fluctuating exchange rates might provide a convenient escape hatch from the above onerous restrictions on Canada's freedom to operate independently, that door also was closed by the inclusion in the declaration of a commitment to move toward greater stability in the exchange markets.

A nation that agrees to all of this cannot be called an independent nation-state. Canada has agreed to all of this. Walter Stewart in *Towers of Gold—Feet of Clay* quotes a Mackenzie King statement of 1935 as saying, "Once a nation parts with the control of its currency and credit, it matters not who makes the nation's laws." Canada's longest-serving prime minister was arguing against the control of the Bank of Canada, resting at that time in the private sector. Re-elected in the fall of 1935, he set in motion the legislation that would place the central bank and monetary policy firmly in the hands of the federal government, or so Mackenzie King thought.

Mr. King argued that the major function of a central bank is to regulate credit and currency in the best interests of the economic life of the nation. And he also believed that the best interests of the country could only be defined by the government of the day, elected by the people in response to the policies and platforms that had been put forward by that government. It certainly did not occur to him when he vigorously debated the Bank of Canada Bill in 1935, or moved the nationalization of the bank in 1938, that technocrats in the Central Bank would, or could, determine where lay the best interests of the Canadian people. It was the King position that the problems facing a nation ultimately and always demand political, not technical, solutions, and monetary issues could not in any way be an exception.

A governor of the Central Bank accepts the mandate, the terms of reference, and the policy directions laid down by the government, or he can resign. The goals of the institution define the range and limits of its operations, and these goals are given by elected governments. If the group of seven industrial nations lays down the policy directions that will bring together interest-rate movement, growth of monetary aggregates, produce co-ordinated fiscal measures to reduce government expenditures and budget deficits, and stabilize exchange rates by controlling rate changes, then where is the freedom of elected governments to address the problems peculiar to their community? And yet this is the situation in which Canada finds itself presently. Can Canada, or even the others, be called independent sovereign states?

Confederation gave some three-and-a-half million Canadians political control over four provinces of British North America. While the Fathers of Confederation would have little faith in an ideological choice to develop the Canadian economy by government action, this option was not available, since none of the three levels of government had the money or credit available through domestic sources necessary to achieve reasonable rates of development.

Alexander Galt and George Brown in particular had pushed for Confederation on the grounds of a Canadian market of three-and-a-half million people, but such a market simply did not exist. Nova Scotia and New Brunswick were within the geographical space of New England manufacturers, and tariff protection could not match the disparity in transportation costs facing the fledgling industry of southern Ontario. Montreal, with its intimate links to metropolitan England and a surrounding province with largely rural, agricultural, and subsistence economies in fact, did not provide that thriving level of demand that would justify investment in large- or even small-scale productive facilities.

The federal government could do little to promote growth of the general economy because it was swept up in the desperate urgency to build the transcontinental links in both the West and East needed to reinforce the political unification. In 1874, for example, we only spent the pitifully small sum of $206,000 in the mining, the forestry, and the fisheries sections of the economy. Megaprojects, then as now, captured the attention of our political leaders.

The provinces were even more feeble instruments of growth than the federal government. In 1874, the seven provinces spent the grand total of $10,000 on promoting mining development and $10,000 on strengthening agricultural production. In addition, the provinces had seen their revenues collapse from a total of $16 million in 1866, the year prior to Confederation, to less than $7 million in 1874, after seven years of settling into the new federal system. Of that $6.7 million, $3.8 million, or 58 per cent of provincial revenues, came in the form of federal subsidies. To underline the utter dependence of the four original provinces in the early years of Confederation, Ontario depended on federal grants for 47 per cent of its current revenue, Quebec for 48 per cent, Nova Scotia for 81 per cent, and New Brunswick for 92 per cent. Thus, provincial intervention to get the economy moving was simply not feasible. Vulnerability and dependence was the lot of the provinces in 1874, and vulnerability and dependence are not conducive to development.

With hindsight, it is still difficult to believe that John A. Macdonald, the Conservative prime minister of Canada, could have adopted any policy other than the so-called American solution, protectionism and the Tariff of 1879. The challenge facing the Fathers of Confederation was to give economic substance and direction to the political structure of the new nation. By 1867, however, Canada was already fully integrated into the continental economy of the United States, for the free movement of persons, capital, and transfers of resource ownership was a daily experience. The complete mobility of factors is a much greater threat to sovereignty and national freedom than free trade in goods and services. In 1867, there was no significant barrier to the mobility of the factors of production, either resources or Canadian manpower. Thus the Macdonald government had to live with a Canada set in its economic ways, a supplier of raw materials to Great Britain until free trade in 1846, and then the supplier of largely the same resources to the United States under the terms of the Reciprocity Treaty of

1854-1866. When this was not renewed, the Canada of 1867 had cause to believe itself isolated and insecure.

Macdonald's tariff was mistimed, a hundred years too soon, by which I mean that it would be a more appropriate policy in 1983 than it was in 1879, when there were few industries and little domestic capital available for entrepreneurs and risk takers, and few Canadian entrepreneurs who remained in the country. In any event, the richer, more rapidly expanding—one could say exploding—American economy was an attraction for the best and brightest in Canada, and the flow of emigration to the south swelled dramatically in the last two decades of the nineteenth century. Our loss, of course, was the American gain.

On the other hand, protectionism in the United States and Germany had worked because there were large markets and mature industries to protect. In Canada, there were no strong industries except the resource and financial sectors. Protectionism is designed to support the infant firm, but given the size of markets, not even the infants that were to be helped by the tariff could advance far beyond their local markets. Internal tariffs and transportation costs quickly limited expansion in an east-west direction, and south-north traffic remained heavy to the benefit of federal customs revenues.

In brief, tariffs protect the strong and the established. They may protect viable infant industries where these exist, but these infant industries should have growing markets that will yield surpluses for reinvestment and further growth, and financial institutions that will be sufficiently imaginative and entrepreneurial themselves to support initiative and risk taking. All these conditions existed in Germany, or were provided by government in the last four decades of the nineteenth century. They all came together during the same period in the United States, a period in which the United States emerged as the most powerful industrial nation in the world. In these conditions, protectionism will work. In the conditions existing in Canada from Confederation to 1900, they did not exist; the dependence of the Canadian economy was firmly established at that time.

The United States' growth rate could not have been sustained in those years without the heavy flow of British capital, but flows were in the form of bonds and debentures placed by the wealthy and their investment trusts. The form of the capital flows was the important difference between the Canadian and the American experience. Canada has been the recipient principally of direct investment funds in its industrial and resource sectors, equity and ownership flows carrying property rights to perpetual streams of income. Thus the equity in and the control of basic sectors of the Canadian economy remained and remain firmly in the hands of foreign investors and entrepreneurs.

The United States, on the other hand, never lost control of its own economy, nor was it drained of the surpluses needed to maintain and expand its productive base after it had redeemed the bonds and debentures on which it had borrowed. It was the American determination to keep control of its own economy that constituted the difference between the two economic policies. The United States grew an economic strength and military power financed by the surpluses that it kept at home.

Confederation had laid down the groundwork for the political control of British North America by the people of Canada, the new nation. With political control assured, the challenge to acquire control of the economy followed. The question is not whether a new nation should or should not acquire control of its own economy, but how it should do so. Political unification would have little significance or meaning if economic control did not come with it. Ideology comes into the equation when the government rules on the method and means of acquiring that economic control. Does the new nation utilize the private sector or the public sector to develop and to expand the economy? And if the private sector, will the major responsibility rest with domestic investment or with foreign investment, or with some combination of both?

The government's choice, in the heyday of laissez faire and unlimited faith in the individual, could only be to rely on the self-interest, efficiency, and profit motivation of the private sector. In practice, however, this meant reliance on the foreign private sector, for there were neither the markets, the domestic capital formation, nor indigenous entrepreneurship of sufficient quality and quantity available to spark the Canadian economy. As a result, Canadian growth languished for an entire generation while the government of Canada, struggling with the finances of railways and other megaprojects to span the continent, had no funds for development, and the provinces struggled to stay afloat on the subsidies provided by the Dominion.

The framers of the tariff policy extolled it as a protectionist measure to preserve the Canadian market for domestic infant industry. They did not realize that a tariff could not possibly ensure national control of an industrial sector in a continental economy—Canada and the United States—where there was already a free movement of persons, capital, services, and goods. A tariff on goods, then, could raise revenues for the federal government, but it could not protect. In fact, imports from the United States, as a percentage of total imports, doubled between 1870 and World War I.

The Canadian experience with continental integration following upon Confederation provides clear evidence that the assumption of a greater wealth upon the allocation of factors of production in a larger market, perhaps even a world market, may be valid, but that there are still bound to be winners and losers. As Canadian resources and people moved southward, the reallocation of these factors of production strengthened the American economy significantly, while leaving Canada weakened by the loss of much of its resource and manpower strength. The mobile Canadians did well as they strengthened and enhanced the growth rate in their new homeland, but at the cost of the stagnating and increasingly dependent economy in the land of their birth. From 1860 until 1900, Canada was not a land of hope and immigration, but a land of frustrated ambition and emigration. This was the period when we set ourselves firmly in the role of economic satellite and suppliers of our resources, our land, and our labour, to the American economy, a role that we still play and that Williamsburg intends us to play in the future.

Given the free movement of Canadian factors of production to the south, what did Macdonald's Tariff of 1879 really accomplish? Basically, it increased the cost of living by reducing the incomes of Canadians, and little else. The tariff was a revenue-gathering device, not a protective instrument. Few of the industries that did exist could qualify as infant industries worthy of protection. They were small, single-product, and community-based firms in a largely barter environment, fully protected by transportation costs and local loyalties, and themselves indifferent to expansion and larger markets. Markets in Canada were not national, as the Fathers of Confederation had vociferously and confidently predicted, but a jumble of separate markets sustained by geographic barriers and transportation costs, plus the fierce regional and cultural loyalties that made market penetration a costly affair.

If the tariff had been effective as a protective measure—that is, if it had succeeded in preserving Canadian markets for Canadian entrepreneurs—one could have expected a flow of the new American branch plants during this period. In fact, there was little direct investment during the next twenty years, indicating that Canadian markets were too small and scattered to justify investment and that the most efficient way to supply the meagre market was still the shipping of American goods, not capital, over the tariff wall.

It was only when the frontier in the United States had been closed that American capital turned its attention northward. Confederation, to repeat, was a political union that never became a nation in control of its own economy. The national policy of 1879, often touted as Canada's declaration of economic independence, was nothing more than a sales tax on the Canadian consumer, a source of revenues to shore up declining customs and excise revenues and to avert national bankruptcy.

A protective tariff appealed to the national sentiment for a protected market and the desire to build a more balanced, diversified—hence less vulnerable—economy. The assumptions were: a) That there was a strong and concentrated market to justify domestic investment and to support industry; b) That there was a sufficient number of infant industries and firms to protect; and c) That a banking and financial community existed, ready and willing to devote resources to the financing of industrial growth in preference to the less risky short-term commercial financing at which they were adept. All three assumptions were mistaken.

The continuing pilgrimages to Washington that are a feature of our own times commenced before Confederation and continued in the years after, as Ottawa strenuously tried to have the Reciprocity Treaty renewed. But it was useless and—from Washington's point of view—unnecessary. They already had all the control over the Canadian economy that they required. More fundamentally, the Fathers of Confederation found the institutions and elements of the Canadian economy to be completely subject to the needs and wants of American market mechanisms. Thus the purpose of political unification—the control of one's land, resources, and capital to achieve an improving standard of living for the people—was beyond them.

The growth of the Canadian economy, then as now, depended on decisions taken elsewhere. Canada was, for all intents and purposes, a market in real estate and raw materials, without large enough markets to throw off surpluses nor domestic capital sufficient to finance a greater share of our own growth.

The course of Canada's dependence on foreign investment took form in the first decade of this century, although the pattern itself had been set well before Confederation. In 1983, Canadian economic dependence is without parallel in the developed world. An analysis of the operations of some 220,000 non-financial corporations in 1980 showed that 36 per cent of the equity ownership and 38 per cent of all the profits in the group accrued to foreign-controlled companies. Such is our present vulnerability to outside pressures.

By comparison, the total sales of foreign subsidiaries in the United States amount to approximately 2 per cent of their GNP. Does the United States take a relaxed view of this 2 per cent direct-investment problem? By no means. The findings of various research groups in the United States are widely publicized and debated in their media, and this has increased the activity of American agencies in the areas of trade and commerce, banking, oil and gas, justice, the securities-and-exchange commission, communications, and defence procurement. In fact, as one consultant has noticed, the scope of United States restrictions on and barriers to foreign investment is so vast that it has taken almost three volumes just to set them out. Very simply, no comparison is to be made between the measures and practices introduced by the United States to restrain a foreign investment that touches only 2 per cent of their gross national product and the single timorous investment-review agency that

Canada has put in place after more than a third of her economy has been found to be in foreign control.

A strategy for greater independence means that the Canadian economy must be switched into new directions—not overnight, since one does not overcome the errors and inertia of more than a century with a brutal turnaround. The damage to the present structure would be immediate and biting. But slowly, perhaps over a generation, we can accomplish new directions that will give an assurance of a more promising and sovereign future.

Sweden faced much the same dilemma, and introduced a policy in 1916 whereby the Swedish parliament insisted that the ownership and control of natural resources, lands and forests, markets and manufacturing must remain firmly in Swedish hands. This policy contains many lessons for Canada. The Swedish government argued, and the people agreed, that to have permitted foreigners to own and control Swedish lands and resources, the life-support system of their economy, would have been detrimental to the interest of the nation. Such a policy would have, of course, made the Swedish consumer vulnerable to exploitation by Swedish manufacturers and industrialists, but Sweden also introduced at the same time a free-trade policy which forced her businessmen to meet world standards of performance. In sum, Swedish economic policy reversed the road taken in Canada by insisting on free trade in goods and limiting the movement of her factors of production.

The beginning of economic wisdom is the control of our own money and credit, as Mackenzie King pointed out. An independent monetary policy does not mean that we can ignore the policies and practices of our neighbour to the south, but it does mean that we do not blindly accept its objectives and policies as our own. We should not be the thirteenth federal branch of its reserve system, nor should we adopt practices in the interest of harmony with the International Monetary Fund at the expense of efforts to resolve domestic problems such as inflation and unemployment. We need to reject the follow-the-leader practices that have kept us dependent for more than a century.

Money and credit policies can force the direction of all other elements of economic planning—fiscal, trade, energy, employment, and industrial—into a monetary framework. A monetary policy totally aligned with that of another nation means that all economic policies will be similarly contained. But a central bank is not responsible for the definition of the best interests of the nation. It is the government, elected by the people, that alone can decide on the economic, political, and social objectives of the community. As an agency, the bank must accept and adapt to the directions laid down by government. It is not the other way around, as is now the case.

No other nation in the world is so controlled by foreign capital and multinational corporations as Canada. The problem posed by the threat of the corporate cathedrals to the processes of democracy are immediate and urgent. One cannot expect nations such as the United States, Japan, and Germany, which benefit from the number of multinationals headquartered in their capitals, to raise questions about the role of these monoliths in the world community. The international legitimation—that is, freedom from national sovereignty—that these commercial giants seek is not an acceptable answer. It will not be tolerated by nations whose objectives of a fair distribution of what is produced in their country, and a rising standard of living for their people, are not compatible with corporate goals of concentration of wealth and power in the private sector.

Philosophically, politically, socially, economically, and culturally, society has yet to examine the awesome impact of these self-determining, self-propelling, perpetual money-making machines. Whether they are foreign owned or not is beside the point. Who is to ask the real questions about corporate growth? To whom are you responsible? To yourselves alone, to the people who own you, to the nations in which you operate? What are your goals and are they ethically justified?

More than any other nation, Canada has a stake in the answers to these questions. Until they are answered, Canada will remain a country that cannot answer the question, who is in charge here?

Chapter
Four

The New Cathedrals

Peter Drucker accurately reflected the euphoria and awe surrounding global corporations when he wrote: "Multinationals, whether corporate or communist, put economic sovereignty ahead of political nationality; the multinational corporation is by far our most effective economic instrument today and probably the one organ of economic development that actually develops. It is the one non-nationalist institution in a world shaken by nationalist delirium. It puts the economic decision beyond the effective reach of the political process and its decision makers, national governments."

However much one may be astonished by Mr. Drucker's eulogy, he speaks what is for many the simple truth. The dominant and dominating institution of our time is the commercial corporation. Few suspected when the act of incorporation for commercial purposes became, in the nineteenth century, a simple right, that the chartered company would ever attain its present importance and strength.

Drucker puts his point of view very well. In essence, he is saying that it is economics that determines the directions that a community should take, because the corporation knows best what are the priority needs and problems facing the nation. The nation-state has become an outmoded and archaic institution unable to deal with the mounting complexities and decisions of the world.

While attempts at military, religious, and revolutionary domination of our social institutions are in fact the history of the Western world, the commercial attack on the role of politics, the open discussion of directions and the possibility of choosing freely, is now the dominant threat to our liberties, as President Eisenhower foresaw.

The heart of the problem lies not in the multinational corporation or the giant conglomerate as such but rather in the concept itself of the corporation as a social institution.

The multinational is not a non-nationalist institution, as Mr. Drucker puts it, but is, in fact, the supreme national instrument of the industrial powers. American economic power is based on hundreds of huge international corporations operating in all corners of the globe. As Mr. Fowler, secretary of the treasury under President Johnson, described them, they were "mighty engines of Enlightened Capitalism." He then went on to declare that "for this nation—the United States—they have not only a commercial importance but a highly significant role in U.S. foreign policy." That is blunt enough! The occasion was the imposition of guidelines on the operations of American subsidiaries in Canada, December, 1965.

To emphasize the point, the secretary went on to say that "much more is involved than the economic advantages of investors of capital and the return to profits." While Canadians have been repeatedly told by their political leaders that the citizenship of those who own and control Canadian resources and Canadian markets is a matter of little or no importance, the secretary of the United States Treasury lays down the doctrine that American multinationals are expected to serve the interests of United States foreign policy. While Canadian economists were teaching that the essence of free enterprise lies in the pursuit of profits and maximizing the return on investment, a member of the U.S. cabinet says not so.

As a colleague of mine, Dr. John Dales of the University of Toronto, pointed out at the time, "We did suppose that American subsidiaries were business enterprises, run by businessmen intent on making a profit. If they really are a herd of little Trojan horses under the control of Washington, economists have nothing to say about them. We know nothing whatever about the behaviour of Trojan horses."

The 1965 imposition of guidelines on subsidiaries of American corporations operating in Canada, while later rescinded, illustrated the extent of Canadian vulnerability to American priorities. In this instance, controlling their balance-of-payments deficits limited United States multinationals, who were told to require their branch plants abroad to import more of their requirements from or through the American parent, to declare larger dividends, and to return excess working capital to the home office. Drucker's point that multinationals put economic sovereignty ahead of political nationality is wrong on two counts. When the United States Department of Commerce orders hundreds of American multinationals to force an expanded repatriation of funds from abroad to reduce the severity of balance-of-payment deficits, we are no longer dealing with the economic sovereignty of multinationals or even with the large numbers of economic theory, but rather with a single, directing political voice—not with the disparate and independent decisions of thousands of businessmen acting in their own corporate interests but with deliberate and hard government policy in Washington. Secondly, it is not economic sovereignty and decision making that rides over the political sovereignty of the host country but the demands and political priorities of the investing nation.

Of even greater concern to Canadians than Mr. Drucker's views should be the attitude of the federal government and its agencies such as the Bank of Canada to the whole question of ownership and control. Briefly, the opinion has always been that, as long as investment funds flow in and incomes are rising, the citizenship of those who own and control major sectors of the Canadian economy does not matter.

With respect to the imposition of the guidelines on Canadian business in December, 1965, there was more resistance from the managements of the Canadian companies (who saw their freedom to buy in the best market and to reinvest funds in such projects as they deemed to be in the best interests of the company dramatically reduced) than there was from their American parents or the Canadian government.

The American parent, of course, could not afford

to antagonize the federal government and the Pentagon, particularly by opposing U.S. policy, given their dependence on the enormous market for goods and services in Washington.

As for the Canadian government and the officials in the Department of Finance, together with the Governor of the Bank of Canada, they did not comprehend in the slightest the significance of this serious infringement of Canadian sovereignty and the national interest. It remained for an American economist, Professor Fritz Machlup of Princeton University, to point out that the introduction of guidelines to control economic activity abroad meant that the "United States has taken an enormous step away from our systems of free enterprise."

Contrary to Mr. Drucker, the world of the multinationals is no longer the world of private capitalism but is, in fact, the world of a guided capitalism wherein the leading industrial governments transform the managements of multinational corporations into lengthened arms of the home governments. It is this consistent invasion of the political authority of the host nations that is creating the hostile environment to the concept of an emerging international organization of production and specialization with consequent political and economic vulnerability for the smaller countries.

When Mr. Drucker speaks of the multinational as "probably the one organ of economic development that actually develops," he is talking nonsense. There is an immediate investment period that gives construction jobs; but the purpose of any investment is to show a profit, i.e., to take out more from a market or an economy than one puts in. In the case of the multinational, a one-time investment of capital, often a minimal contribution, has secured control of a resource or a share of a market with the rights to an indefinite flow of income arising therefrom. Investment by the multinational takes place only when the opportunity exists to take more out of an economy than is put in. A multinational pursues the surplus in any situation and leaves the social problems to governments.

Equity flows of foreign capital with absolute and perpetual rights to future surpluses drain the recipient nation of the very sums needed to maintain and to expand its own economy. The objective of each investment is to take out of the zone of operations more than has been committed, and inevitably the investing nations expand at the expense of the less-developed ones. More importantly, since the debtor nations have sold the control of future as well as the present streams of revenue to their creditors, they never do get back control of their economies.

When the Kennedy administration conducted hearings in 1961 on tax recommendations governing the operations of global companies, hundreds of pages of testimony proved the point that the United States multinationals brought back far greater sums than they invested abroad. Thus Standard Oil of New Jersey had a cumulative surplus of $1.5 billion over a five-year period. Procter and Gamble, during a ten-year period, sent abroad $11 million and brought back to the United States $290 million. And on and on.

Once established and in control of a market share or a resource endowment, the subsidiary is in a position to exert the power that comes from the property rights that it has acquired, for property is sovereignty and the right to income flows. Sovereignty over its activities enables the foreign corporation to insist on the laws, privileges, and concessions necessary to encourage its expansion and control.

Everyone agrees to the free flow of international capital and particularly to developing nations. In its equity form, however, the absolute ownership and property rights attached to their investments enable multinationals to accumulate the surpluses out of each market in which they operate and to dispose of them as they will. Thus a minimal income to labour may remain in the host nation, but the surpluses such as royalty and management fees, interest, dividends, and retained earnings accrue to the creditor nation through its multinational firms.

To declare, as Drucker does, that multinationals put economic sovereignty ahead of political nationality is to assert that the nation has lost all power to limit the rights of private property in the interests of the conservation of exhaustible resources, and the provision of social services such as education, health, welfare, and acceptable working conditions based on the reconciliation of the needs of future generations with the greed for immediate capital gains. But this cannot endure; it invites growing hostility and the certain destruction of the multinational system as we know it.

The dominance of multinationals begins initially with the exploitation of their domestic markets and the consequent accumulation of surpluses. Capacity soon comes to exceed domestic markets and, eventually, the export markets that are not protected by effective tariffs and quotas. One could ask whether the excess capacity was not bad investment and suggest that the funds might have been better distributed to share owners in the home country who could pursue their own consumption and investment patterns. But the capital is retained and moved abroad as direct investment to capture the protected markets for the same technology. The technology that is exported is the technology of the advanced economy. It has to be because the parent, denied the profits on the export of final products, is looking for the profits inherent in the export of the same basic raw materials, equipment, and component parts that it has produced to satisfy its domestic market.

Cosmocorps, then, do transfer advanced technology widely. But a suitable technology for a highly industrialized nation may not be and likely will not be appropriate for a developing nation. The supply of the factors of production in the two economies will certainly not be the same. In the more advanced home economy, capital will be more abundant and its price cheaper, while labour will be relatively scarce and wages much higher than in the developing nation. The transfer of a technology based on a high capital-output ratio to an economy where capital is scarce and expensive and ignores the employment of the labour that is abundant and cheap distorts the pattern of growth and is bad economics, however advanced the technology. As Professor Schumpeter has stated, "This explains why technically backward methods of production may still be the most rational ones, provided the more perfect methods would require less of a plentiful factor and more of one which is less plentiful, and why the technically most perfect method of production is so often a failure in economic life." As Keith Marsden has pointed out, it would be easy to substitute a high-technology bakery employing 60 workers at double their daily wage for traditional methods in West Africa, thereby rendering redundant 565 workers, but the burden of caring for and finding employment for the displaced labour falls upon the economy.

Slower and steadier improvement of existing technologies in the backward nations would enable all sectors of such an economy to advance in concert, but this is not what the multinational has to sell.

The global corporation sells mass-production techniques, even in their branch-plant version. To be profitable, however, mass production requires mass consumption—that is, the homogenization of the tastes, needs, values, and priorities of all the nations within which the firm and its subsidiaries operate. In the name of technical efficiency, we erase the differences among persons, the style and the art of their living. People of different cultures and nations in varying stages of development are made, through enormous selling and advertising pressures, to want the same things. The freedom of the individual to choose, to maintain his own preferences, and to search for satisfaction, is reduced. So it is with nations. If their governments believe that their resources, human and material, are appropriated and applied to objectives other than those of their own choosing, on whom do they turn? The end results are easily foreseen, and therein lies the tragedy. The developing nations will inevitably reject the final and complete Americanization, Japanization, or Europeanization of their economies. The multinationals, as the vehicles of that domination, must face at best control of their operations, if not expropriation. And this brings the governments of the powerful industrial economies, determined to protect the wealth of their corporate citizens, into open conflict with the developing nation-states.

The multinational does not transfer ownership of its methods and technology in its foreign activities. There is no export or sale of these assets to an arms-length entity in the host country. The specific advantage, together with the invested capital, remains the property of the parent as the parent absorbs foreign assets—resources and/or markets—via its branch plants. What happens is not a transfer but an extension of the firm's existing property rights and control over a stream of revenues to new markets and political jurisdictions. The theorist of international resource allocation and the multinational president then assert, without proof or demonstration, that there is a superior efficiency in this global allocation and investment of resources, which must be protected from the political interference of national governments acting in the name of the interests and priorities of their citizens. If the nation-state is to have no place in the board rooms of the global corporation, then the community is indeed in the grip of an industrial autarchy.

The use of the corporate form for commercial purposes is a late product of the Industrial Revolution. We tend to think of the concept of the corporation as an ancient form of organizing business activity, whereas in fact the legislation creating limited companies in Great Britain dates back to 1855 and 1856. The Industrial Revolution had changed economies from the emphasis on agricultural to commercial and industrial activity, with the consequent changing composition of assets and private wealth from land to liquid and current assets. More formal procedures of accounting and administration were clearly needed to protect property. Since the corporate form had been used for centuries to coordinate and control non-profit-making activities—monasteries, bishoprics, universities, highways and canals—its adoption by commercial profit-making activity seemed a natural move. Few could foresee at the time the extent to which the corporate form would be used for the making and accumulating of profit.

In a famous case relating to the responsibilities of the Board of Regents of Dartmouth College, Chief Justice Marshall of the U.S. Supreme Court had defined, in 1819, a corporation as "an artificial being, . . . possessing among its most important properties immortality and individuality, properties by which a perpetual succession of many persons are considered as the same, and may act as an individual."

Until the nineteenth century, incorporation had been a privilege granted by the Crown or state for achieving national purposes or social objectives, privileges that could be and often were taken away. Social institutions—universities, for example—are continually called upon to justify their stewardship and so to continue their work long after the original founders have left the scene. The existence of the institution and the validity of the institution are continually legitimated by the interlock of their services with the objectives of the community. The immortality of the social institution was and is a contingent immortality, conditional on serving the public welfare.

The attributes of the public corporation—continuity, personality, and individuality—were not extended to the private corporation until the Industrial Revolution was well under way. From Adam Smith through to John Stuart Mill writing in 1849, economists viewed the firm as a proprietorship or partnership, mortal like the owners and operators, certain to disappear in time, thus providing the openings for new men, new initiatives, new ideas. If entry was not easy, exit at least was certain. It was this constant turnover in a dynamic, evolving economy that theoretically prevented a large number of firms from controlling prices and production. This is not the appropriate manner of looking at the economy of 1983 or the multinational, although the model still survives in economic theory.

A commercial corporation may be endowed by the law with immortality, but somehow this attribute has to be supported by adequate sources of funds. Unlike universities or bishoprics, which depend on gifts and alms from their supporters, or municipalities and states, which depend on taxes, the commercial corporation can only prove its claim and right to perpetual operations by gaining and maintaining a control over consumer markets and/or natural resources. Such a control or near monopoly will enable it to survive more confidently through time, growing and accumulating all the way.

The half century after the passage of the limited-liability and corporate legislation saw an unprecedented concentration of industrial power that led to consolidations, mergers, and trusts. The Sherman Act, designed to slow down concentration and the creation of trusts, was rendered virtually harmless by an act of the New Jersey legislature in 1888 that permitted corporations to buy each other out, a movement that reappears regularly as takeovers and consolidations reach billion-dollar proportions in 1983.

Their control of their markets, their absolute size (measured by assets and material strength), and their independence from those who own them means that society has created institutions that can grow without limit through time. As they grow, they burst through national boundaries and demand the right to range across the world—anonymous institutions that acknowledge no citizenship and would be free of all responsibility except the single objective of accumulating wealth.

In 1970, the Royal Bank of Canada was a hundred years old and had accumulated $11.4 billion in assets. Twelve years later, in 1982, its wealth and power had increased to $88.5 billion.

The CPR, founded in 1880, by 1970 reported assets of $2.3 billion. By 1982, its assets has risen to $17.3 billion, partly financed by government generosity permitting the deferral of $1.8 billion in corporate tax.

Imperial Oil was founded in 1880 and had collected assets of $1.6 billion by 1970. By 1982, with the federal government amiably deferring the payment of $1.3 billion in taxes, Imperial Oil had amassed the grand total of $7.5 billion in assets.

Corporate capitalism is not a competitive system when 608 corporations reported taxable income of $15.5 billion in 1980, 53 per cent of the taxable income of the $29.5 billion reported by the Canadian corporate community of 451,567 firms. These are the firms that administer prices in their markets, control output of goods and services, and generate the funds from their operations that ensure the "immortality" that the law accepts.

A government can be dismissed by voters, a church affected by the scepticism of its adherents, or a university deserted by a community for losing touch with its needs or goals. Each of these institutions is bound by the purposes and priorities of its constituents.

The sole concern of the corporation, however, is with itself. Being a new legal person, it is possessed of an identity and form that is distinct from that of the people who own it, who work in it, and who deal with it. What happens to the corporation if a number of shareholders decide to sell their shares? Nothing. Others take their place through the facilities of the stock exchanges; management, which considers owners to be speculating in and outers, is indifferent to the change.

Managements come and go as do the workers. There is a little ceremony, a wristwatch, or a television set. The corporation, of which these men and women were a part, carries on undisturbed. The whole is not only greater than the sum of its parts—owners, management, workers—it is completely separate from any of them. If the corporation is linked to anything, it is not to people.

In 1973 Barclays Bank Limited of London, England, had a record year, a gross profit of £199 million. The chairman, in an advertisement in the *Economist*, announced that £96 million would be retained by the bank to increase the wool on its back, that £88 million had to go to the government for taxes, and £15 million in dividends to the stockholders. He stated: "It is also worth recording that of the three parties who make up a bank, namely stockholders, staff, and customers, none has gained much from these profits." And, indeed, they had not. In a year of 10 per cent inflation, the salary increases were limited to 7 per cent, the dividend increase to 5 per cent, and customers had to pay higher rates of interest.

These facts apply right across the corporate spectrum. The Barclays chairman was simply being frank. The corporation has simply one concern, to make full provision for its own continuity and growth.

Corporations have become ends in themselves when they were never meant to be more than efficient means of grouping the factors of production, land, and labour with the support and thrust of capital saved, to expand the output of goods and services and thus establish a higher standard of living for the whole community.

Unwilling to accept the goals of those who own it—although private property is the core of the value system in which it flourishes—struggling to free itself from the priorities and purposes of the community, the sole concern of the corporation is with its future. Self-perpetuating, self-determining, independent of time and space, the object of the corporation's existence is itself.

To be wealthy, said Aristotle, is no problem, even for a philosopher. He related the story of Thales, the astronomer-philosopher born in Miletus. Observing the stars, the philosopher judged the conditions appropriate for a great olive harvest. Whereupon Thales bought up all the olive presses in Chios and Miletus. There was a great harvest, but no olive presses—except those belonging to the philosopher, who rented them out at prices that soon made him rich. Control a market, be a monopolist.

Aristotle told another story. A man in Sicily bought up all the iron that was available. When merchants came to buy, he was the only seller, and with little difficulty he soon gained 200 per cent. Dionysius, the tyrant of Syracuse, called the man before him and told him that he could keep his money but that he must leave Syracuse. Dionysius feared that the man's wealth would soon be dangerous to his own political authority.

Aristotle established clearly the supremacy of politics over economics. Dionysius, wrote Aristotle approvingly, had recognized immediately and clearly that the accumulation of wealth can be a threat to and victor over political authority. For Aristotle, politics—even when practised by a tyrant—was to be preferred to the tyranny of wealth, for it is by politics that people decide on their priorities and their future directions.

Laissez faire was the spirit of the age when the acts of incorporation were adopted, permitting the right to incorporate with a freedom and lack of control that was clearly irresponsible. One hundred and twenty-seven years later, society is still paying for its failure to impose safeguards, to define responsibility, and to make accountable to the state the new means of organizing industrial activity to produce a greater wealth.

When forms of business organization were personal—partnerships or proprietorships—there was no problem about defining business ethics. Business ethics were personal ethics, and the ethics of the person may be described by the one word—"love." "Have and do whatsoever thou wilt," was the commandment of St. Augustine, but he was not inviting anarchy. A true love would not infringe the rights of others, and this boundary to one's actions preserves community and freedom.

To command a corporation to love would be madness. Commanding a corporation to love would be asking it to distribute its wealth, to commit suicide. On the other hand, the corporation cannot be concerned simply with itself; it cannot be the object of its existence. It can and must be forced to conduct itself so that its activities correspond with the aims of the community, with the state itself as the seat of power and elected spokesman of the people.

Chapter
Five

What Can Politics Do?

I have made great use of the commitments made at the Williamsburg conference by the leaders of the seven industrial nations relating to the common defense of the West and the need to achieve comergence—i.e., integration of economic policies, particularly in the monetary, fiscal, and exchange-rate fields. The summit statements are the clearest and most comprehensive description of what has been taking place in the West, the putting in place of an informal supranational authority which could integrate the foreign-policy posture, the defence contributions, and the economic policies of the Western powers.

To repeat the substance of the decisions, the leaders of the seven leading industrial nations agreed:

1. In the statement on arms control: "We shall maintain sufficient military strength to deter any attack, to counter any threat, and to ensure the peace." Also, "The security of our countries

is indivisible and must be approached on a global basis."

2. In the text on economic recovery: "To promote convergence of economic performance in our economies" and "focusing on near-term policy actions leading to convergence in the medium-term." This goal was to be reached by following a pattern of non-inflationary growth of the money supply, appropriate interest rates, discipline over government expenditures, and convergence of exchange rates.

Williamsburg gives the impression that a community of the West has been created with authority over the participating nation-states. In fact, the leaders could do no more than agree to follow certain lines of conduct that would contribute to national and group security and to follow this up with appropriate economic initiatives.

Williamsburg as an exercise in public relations may or may not impress the Russians with the display of solidarity, but no international legal organization was created that could strip away elements of national sovereignty and so provide the unification that exists in the Soviet bloc. Not one of the Western leaders would have dared to accept openly the limitations of their sovereignty spelled out in the agreed press releases if these limitations were to be enshrined in an international treaty. It is worth repeating that the legal sovereignty of a state is incompatible with the existence of a supra-national authority that has a power centre of its own. A legal space is a universal space, although sovereign nations may choose not to exercise their rights in given situations. To the self-limitation of its sovereignty, Canada has been particularly prone.

Williamsburg did do something, and that something was to establish a political, but not a legal, power centre which integrated the military and economic strengths of all seven nations and directed this accumulation of power to the turning back of the Russian threat—the priority purpose of the informal, political union. This priority of the bloc immediately assumed pride of place over the internal needs of the individual member nations, whose citizens were counselled to lower their expectations and to bear the burdens of unemployment and inflation a little longer.

It is to be emphasized that the Williamsburg agreements are not binding on the nations involved, for the voluntary agreements can be reversed at any time that national interests may dictate. Nor are the Williamsburg agreements a step forward in the quest for world order and peace, because the conference did not bring forward that set of moral principles and postulates that might serve as the basis for a true international authority, founded on the sovereignty of nations that is limited only by their respect for the freedom and self-determination of other nations.

The unifying forces at Williamsburg were two: sixteen thousand nuclear warheads in the arsenal of the United States, and the material interest of the six satellites in keeping open the huge markets of the United States. To possess power is to wield it, openly, and brutally or quietly, but firmly. Canada has the sovereign right to refuse to test the Cruise, but our political leaders know the economic costs and recoiled before the consequences. For the Europeans, the economic sovereignty lost is deemed a small price to pay for the security of the nuclear umbrella and the American pledge to safeguard the security of Western Europe as its own. Given the growing demonstrations against the deployment of the nuclear missiles in Europe, the summit leaders may yet find the cost in political instability to be very high.

It is not in the American interest to keep the impassioned rhetoric alive—the evil of the East and the goodness of the West—thus creating the conditions of uncertainty and fear that will accelerate the pace of economic integration, and build a new Western economy composed of the resources of North America, Europe, and Japan with free movement of factors into and out of the United States heartland. So sweeping a unification of the Western economies, for the purpose of accumulating military and productive power, leads to the frustration of a constantly receding parity with an equally determined foe. There is no national security for either side in numbers, for parity at the level of a nuclear holocaust existed when each side possessed a thousand nuclear warheads. When today each side possesses sixteen thousand missiles, there is still parity and still the threat of holocaust—two republics of insects and ash.

For Canada the agreements reached at Williamsburg are simply more of the same. The three most sensitive areas for a nation jealous of its sovereignty are bound to be the areas of its relations with foreign countries, its defence arrangements, and its control of its money and credit. In all three areas, Canada agreed to follow the policy directions laid down by President Reagan and so confirmed again, for all the world to note, our membership in the American empire.

Until the British conversion to Free Trade in 1846, the Canadian colonies were content to be suppliers of raw materials to the mother country. After the withdrawal of British preferences, Canada sought and was granted reciprocity with the United States in 1854. When the treaty lapsed in 1865, Canada remained a supplier of resources and importer of manufactured goods, an integrated member of the continent economy. Canada did not so much lose her independence as choose not to exercise it.

Canadian independence would have required some show of control over our resources, the land, the people, and the capital arising therefrom as well as the markets for goods and services and the surpluses they yielded. But all this was as freely available to Americans as to Canadians. And similarly with American resources and markets which were as open to the initiative, imagination, and drive of young Canadian entrepreneurs as to their own citizens. There were tariffs, but these were no more than excises, inland duties collected to finance railways and industrial expansion. From the beginning of Confederation, Canada was part of an economy in which the factors of production moved freely and goods did so with a slight surtax, an economic union that has just stopped short of full political unification.

As for defence, the Monroe doctrine applied to Canada as much as to any other nation in the Americas—at least as far as the United States was concerned, and that was all that counted. When it came to foreign affairs, we were taken for granted by foreign powers, who rightly assumed that we would follow the policies either of the motherland or the rich neighbour to the south. To most nations, friendly as they were, we were considered passive, even faceless, and seldom with a contribution to make. Canada did not have a minister of external affairs until 1946, a condition that served to emphasize our slow maturing as a nation.

I take the Williamsburg economic declaration for what it is, a clear and unequivocal request that Canada integrate its economic policies with those of the United States and adapt its resources to operate in a unified market system. Accepting this demand means that we make U.S. purposes and goals our purposes and goals, and their priorities our priorities. We give up the possibility of providing a framework in which a free and independent Canadian society may be built. If we are forced to accept as our own the objectives of other nations pursuing military superiority and nuclear supremacy, we have no right to call ourselves a nation. I prefer to believe that we are a nation, that we can follow a more independent course, and that we have the objective of greater employment for our people and an improved standard of living for the less fortunate in our nation.

Canada is at a crossroads. Our major market, the United States, can no longer afford free trade. If the United States operated in a fully free-trade environment, their trade deficit would be well beyond the $70 billion projected for this year. Worse, basic industries such as steel, heavy equipment, cars—the very core of a defence posture—would quickly collapse. Since this is unthinkable, it is obvious that the U.S. will become increasingly protectionist and press down more heavily on export markets such as our own.

Canadian history is a story of long-lived reliance on the export of natural resources. New sources in South America and Africa, with lower labour costs, are the competitors that are closing down our mines and refineries. As well, many of these nations have no other means of paying down their huge debts and interest charges than by increasing the volume of raw-material exports to the industrial West, thus earning the foreign exchange necessary to meet their commitments.

It is obvious that new directions are being imposed on us as the foundations of traditional economic policy, resource exploitation, and capital imports are crumbling beneath us. The decisions that we make in the eighties will make us a satellite economy operating on the fringes of the American empire unless we take stock of ourselves, our institutions, our human and material resources and resolve to put in place the political and economic structures that will provide us with the means and time to effect an evolving self-transformation.

It is time that Canada affirmed her independence as a sovereign state. We are not an accident of geography, nor are our traditions, culture, and languages to be written off in the alleged efficiency of a global economy. Nor can we yield control of our markets and means of production to others in the pursuit of some pseudo-internationalism.

I am not arguing against the possibility and hope in a great human family. I am simply saying that such an achievement, if it does come, will be an affair of the heart, the mind, and the spirit, not the result of organizing production on a world scale that maximizes skyscraper wealth, corporate cathedrals, and capital accumulation, leaves labour alone in the market place, and ends in the global homogenization of consumption and cultural patterns. The promise by globalists of a greater gross world product that would provide a rising standard of living for all people is an illusion and thoroughly dishonest.

Every nation must, if it is to satisfy the desires and needs of its citizens, have control of its economy. If the resources and the revenues from markets and production accrue largely to others, then the nation becomes dependent and vulnerable. An economy as a support system must also provide the non-exchange activities of a community, the universities, hospitals, cultural and social purposes, the spiritual elements that define a state as resting, not on material power alone, but on a system of moral values, intellectual freedom, and social responsibility.

A nation must believe in itself, or the worth of its people will never be realized. A nation must take, as its fundamental priority, responsibility for the welfare and standard of living of its people. We cannot accept the optimism and belief of the nineteenth century in a natural order built upon the creativity and enterprise of the individual. Nor can we believe that the vast conglomerates of the twentieth century have anything other than their own accumulations of power and wealth as goals.

As it applies to Canada, the Williamsburg continental integration signifies not only the placing of all our resources, physical and human, at the disposal of the American heartland, but would force the subordination of Canadian policies and interests to the objectives of the Western bloc. Military security in a nuclear world demands alliances and formal agreements. It does not require the subordination and subjugation of friends and allies. Canada's sovereignty demands that she be treated as an ally, not a satellite.

The nation-state is not through as an economic unit nor is it in decline because of the revolution in transportation and communication facilities. The so-called family of nations is a noble idea, but it is not, as Hegel pointed out, a reality. For centuries past, nations have been sensitive to the possible accession to power of the military forces and religious systems that even now control many parts of the world. The democratic nations of the West, however, have avoided these threats, which bring to power an authoritarian militarism or an unyielding fanaticism.

And yet we in the West are witnessing—quietly at first but now with an accelerating pressure—the increasing dominance and power of the commercial and industrial giants over our political institutions, a condition that will inevitably lead to a dictatorship of the left or right. A General Eisenhower warned of it, a Prime Minister Trudeau admits it.

The disarray in modern society comes from the argument that the sovereignty of the nation-state restrains the growth and efficiency of the corporation. Therefore the corporation must be freed from the control of the state, for only in this fashion can it take advantage of its true potential, size, economies of scale, and extended horizons.

It is clear that the nation-state and the corporation are operating on different levels. The corporation maximizes its own future, its own growth. For the nation-state, the heart of the economic system must be the distribution of what is produced in the nation, the power of the society to consume equalling its power to produce. The logic of the corporation is to grow, the responsibility of the state is to achieve a fair distribution. And so the conflict continues, because there is no moral consensus on what is fair, only the illusion that all nations must encourage bigness if they are to share in tomorrow's alleged plenty—for the love affair with bigness is the sentiment that the future will be better.

It is as Uncle Ernst says in *Howard's End*: "It is the vice of a vulgar mind to be thrilled by bigness, to think that a thousand square miles are a thousand times more wonderful than one square mile, and that a million square miles are almost the same as heaven. That is not imagination. It kills it."

To think that a world is better than a hundred nation-states—or a thousand—is an illusion. There could be no single, most efficient application of the world's resources unless there were a single interest, but there is no single goal, or set of goals, to which such an application may be divided. The goals and aims of people are as varied and diverse as there are regions and communities and coalitions within the nation. In other words, choices and allocations are made through the processes of politics, which is the market place through which infinite needs and wants are given their priority and importance. In a democratic society, it is the political decision that, for better or for worse, ends the bureaucratic quibbling, silences the squalling screams for privilege and preference, and alone can provide the order and stability which will protect the individual in a world of conflicting claims and incessant struggles for power.

The nation-state is not in decline. It remains rooted in the soil and the hearts of its people. For a period after the Second World War there was an excessive internationalism that saw the rise of bureaucratic organizations such as NATO, OECD, GATT, and the United Nations itself, which sought to practise sovereignty without the basic element of authority, the power to enforce. Thus the United States ignores the condemnation of GATT for its DISC program, France pulls its forces out of NATO, and members are blandly indifferent to the boring nostrums of the OECD. These organizations can fulminate, they can recommend, but they have no power of their own.

For a generation, Canada has accepted the limitation of its sovereignty by these international organizations in the interests of establishing firm standards of international conduct. When all goes well, there is a disposition to accept the costs, but when unemployment soars and the claims of international bodies erode the sovereignty of the nation-state, the period of self-limitation of state powers is bound to come to a close.

National sovereignty and international authority cannot exist together. The danger of Williamsburg is that Canada accepts informally—for reasons of economic retaliation, political pressures, or balance-of-power tactics—what cannot be put into place legally. There can only be one legal order in Canada that may be flouted by a dominant and brutalizing neighbour. But there cannot be two legal bodies occupying the same space.

Let us be clear on this. Canada is sovereign, but we can be craven because we fear the economic sanctions and the loss of affluence that we now enjoy. This fear may have a foundation in reality. On the other hand, it is at least possible that what we fear is merely fear itself.

In any event, Canada has no choice. It cannot maintain the role of purveyor of raw materials for the simple reason that too many less-developed nations are taking over our markets with lower costs. We simply have to enlarge and diversify our industrial strength. There can be no question that the multinational corporation must adapt to the priorities and policies of the nation in which it operates as developer of resources, processor of goods, and supplier to markets. National policies do not conform to the motivations and objectives of the corporations that the state has admitted to the economy; it is the other way around. And this applies to domestic as well as multinational companies.

In a world in which the pressure on resources is growing from the two directions of, on the one hand, increasing demand with growing populations and rising standards of living and, on the other hand, the significant exhaustion of resources, it becomes evident that the private sector, motivated by its own growth, cannot be the final arbiter and allocator of resources between the corners of the earth, between consumption for today or investment for tomorrow, between the poor and the rich nations.

Limited sovereignty is not sovereignty at all. Hence, no nation can permit the corporation, domestic or multinational, to operate beyond the legal reach of its law. The sovereignty of the state demands that it maintain and secure the control of its own economy, the life-support system of its citizens. Canada has surrendered the value of too large a percentage of its lands, resources, and markets to corporations that have demanded the rights and privileges of absolute ownership as a condition of investment.

As the United States becomes increasingly protectionist, Canada will become increasingly isolated. In fact, it will become not only isolated but vulnerable, as Canadians realize that imported technology and ideas do not create new comparative advantages and that tariff protection does not foster an improved standard of living or allow infant industries time to grow.

Similarly, the emphasis on the export of natural resources before the competition of new nations financed by flows of foreign, including Canadian, capital. It is time that we left the field to the new arrivals of the third world.

New economic policies intend a change in direction, the switch from former ways into new paths. The costs become immediately apparent as change forces adaptation, offends the pride of policy makers, and disrupts ancient investment patterns. The benefits are in the future, but the costs are here and now—individually, corporately, and politically.

The new policies must come down hard on the old failures. Foreign capital never claimed to be a panacea for all our weaknesses. It was we who thought so. We forgot that foreign capital could not make up for the sale and export of our wealth and the emigration of our youth. We did not have enough control of ourselves or our economy to realize that, first and above all else, capital must be made and must be retained at home. By giving away the value of our resources, we never could accumulate the surpluses that would have enabled us to finance and invest in the balanced growth of the

Canadian economy.

What can politics do? First, it must accept the responsibility of sovereignty and the supremacy of politics in deciding the allocation of resources and the directions of future development. Let the economists decide the application and costs of the directions chosen. Secondly, Canada can grow and be of value to the world and to itself only by being an independent, sovereign state, and it can do this only by the control of its own economy and politics.

The ultimate norms directing Canadian policies cannot be the interests of other nations, no matter how powerful, or the fear of their reprisals. Our aims will be truly Canadian when they arise out of the hearts and minds of our people, not when they are dictated at summit conferences or by ambassadorial pressures.

Our political leaders have much to work with. Not only the lands and people which we have always had, but the same burning desire that led so many Canadians to look for challenge elsewhere exists in today's generation. We have all the means to create a viable and gainful economy if we can find the leadership to put it all together.

A nation has an inner structure and vitality that imposes a pattern on its environment. Understanding and having confidence in the spirit and capacity of a people is an essential quality of sound political leadership.

Rene Dubos, in his book *A God Within: A Positive Philosophy for a More Complete Fulfillment of the Human Potential*, quotes Michelangelo expressing his feelings on looking at a block of marble:

The best of artists has that thought alone,
Which is contained within the marble shell.
The sculptor's hand can only break the spell,
To free the figures slumbering in the stone.

The potential and the capacity of Canadians to do great things in and for the world is there. It needs the political leadership and a belief in ourselves to break the spell.

The challenge facing our political leaders is to establish a clear and distinct Canadian identity as an independent state, a worthy ally, but an unwilling satellite.

An identity is clear when our policies, whether in the fields of trade and commerce, external affairs and defence, work in the same direction; an identity is independent when we have control of our own economy, money and credit; it is distinct when Canadian national interests and objectives, with full regard for the interests and choices of others, alone determine our attitudes.

Appendices

Appendices

Appendix A

Summit Statement on Arms Control Joint Communique

Williamsburg, Virginia — May 29, 1983

1. As leaders of our seven countries, it is our first duty to defend the freedom and justice on which our democracies are based. To this end, we shall maintain sufficient military strength to deter any attack, to counter any threat, and to ensure the peace. Our arms will never be used except in response to aggression.

2. We wish to achieve lower levels of arms through serious arms control negotiations. With this statement, we reaffirm our dedication to the search for peace and meaningful arms reductions. We are ready to work with the Soviet Union to this purpose and call upon the Soviet Union to work with us.

3. Effective arms control agreements must be based on the principle of equality and must be veri-

fiable. Proposals have been put forward from the Western side to achieve positive results in various international negotiations: on strategic weapons (S.T.A.R.T.), on intermediate-range nuclear missiles (INF), on chemical weapons, on reduction of forces in Central Europe (MBFR), and a conference on disarmament in Europe (CDE).

4. We believe that we must continue to pursue these negotiations with impetus and urgency. In the area of INF, in particular, we call upon the Soviet Union to contribute constructively to the success of the negotiations. Attempts to divide the West by proposing inclusion of the deterrent forces of third countries, such as those of France and the United Kingdom, will fail. Consideration of these systems has no place in the INF negotiations.

5. Our nations express the strong wish that a balanced INF agreement be reached shortly. It is well known that should this not occur, the countries concerned will proceed with the planned deployment of the U.S. systems in Europe at the end of 1983.

6. Our nations are united in efforts for arms reductions and will continue to carry out thorough and intensive consultations. The security of our countries is indivisible and must be approached on a global basis. Attempts to avoid serious negotiation by seeking to influence public opinion in our countries will fail.

7. We commit ourselves to devote our full political resources to reducing the threat of war. We have a vision of a world in which the shadow of war has been lifted from all mankind, and we are determined to pursue that vision.

Appendix B

Summit Statement on Economic Recovery

Joint Communique announced by President Reagan

Williamsburg, Virginia — May 30, 1983

Our nations are united in their dedication to democracy, individual freedom, creativity, moral purpose, human dignity and personal and cultural development.

It is to preserve, sustain and extend these shared values that our prosperity is important.

The recession has put our societies through a severe test, but they have proven resilient. Significant success has been achieved in reducing inflation and interest rates, there have been improvements in productivity and we now clearly can see signs of recovery.

Nevertheless, the industrialized democracies continue to face the challenge of insuring that the recovery materializes and endures, in order to reverse a decade of cumulative inflation and reduce unemployment, we must all focus on achieving and maintaining low inflation and reducing interest rates from their present too high levels. We renew our commitment to reduce structural budget deficits, in particular by limiting the growth of expenditures.

We recognize that we must act together and that we must pursue a balanced set of policies that take into account and exploit relationships between growth, trade and finance in order that recovery may spread to all countries, developed and developing alike.

In pursuance of these objectives we have agreed as follows:

(1) Our governments will pursue appropriate monetary and budgetary policies that will be conducive to low inflation, reduced interest rates, higher productive investment and greater employment opportunities, particularly for the young.

(2) The consultation process initiated at Versailles will be enhanced to promote convergence of economic performance in our economies and greater stability of exchange rates on the lines indicated in an annex to this declaration. We agree to pursue closer consultations on policies affecting exchange markets and on market conditions. While retaining our freedom to operate independently, we are willing to undertake coordinated intervention in exchange markets in instances where it is agreed where such intervention would be helpful.

(3) We commit ourselves to halt protectionism and, as recovery proceeds, to reverse it by dismantling trade barriers. We intend to consult in appropriate existing fora on ways to implement and monitor this

commitment. We shall give impetus to resolving current trade problems. We will actively pursue the current work programs in the General Agreement on Tariffs and Trade (GATT) and Organization for Economic Cooperation and Development, including trade in services and high technology products. We should work to achieve further trade liberalization negotiations in the GATT with particular emphasis in expanding trade with, and among, developing countries. We have agreed to continue consultations on proposals for a new negotiating round in the GATT.

(4) We view with concern the international financial situation and especially the debt burdens of many developing nations. We agree to a strategy based on effective adjustment and development policies by debtor nations, adequate private and official financing, more open markets and world wide economic recovery. We will seek ratification of the increases in resources for the International Monetary Fund and the general agreements to borrow. We encourage closer cooperation and timely sharing of information among countries and the international institutions in particular, between the International Monetary Fund (IMF), the International Bank for Reconstruction and Development (IBRD), and the GATT.

(5) We have invited ministers of finance in consultation with the managing director of the IMF to define the conditions for improving the international monetary system and to consider the part which might, in due course, be played in this process by a high level, international, monetary conference.

(6) The weight of the recession has fallen very heavily on developing countries and we are deeply con-

cerned about their recovery. Restoring sound economic growth while keeping our markets open is crucial. Special attention will be given to the flow of resources, in particular, official development assistance to poorer countries, and for food and energy production, both bilaterally and through appropriate international institutions. We reaffirm our commitments to provide agreed funding levels for the International Development Agency. We welcome the openness to dialogue which the developing countries evinced at the recent conferences of the non-aligned movement in New Delhi and the Group of 77 in Buenos Aires and we share their commitment to engage with understanding and cooperation in the forthcoming meeting of the United Nations conference on trade and development in Belgrade.

(7) We are agreed upon the need to encourage both the development of advanced technology and the public acceptance of its role in promoting growth, employment and trade. We have noted with approval the report of the Working Group on Technology, Growth and Employment, which was set up at Versailles last year and commend the progress made in the eighteen cooperative projects discussed in that report. We will follow the implementation and coordination of work on these projects and look forward to receiving a further report at our next meeting.

(8) We all share the view that more predictability and less volatility in oil prices would be helpful to world economic prospects. We agreed that the fall in oil prices in no way diminishes the importance and urgency of efforts to conserve energy, to develop economic alternative energy sources, to maintain and where possible

improve contacts between oil-exporting and importing countries, and to encourage the growth of indigenous energy production in developing countries which at present lack it.

(9) East-West economic relations should be compatible with our security interests. We take note with approval of the work of the multilateral organizations which have in recent months analyzed and drawn conclusions regarding the key aspects of East-West economic relations. We encourage continuing work by these organizations as appropriate.

(10) We have agreed to strengthen cooperation in protection of the environment, in better use of natural resources and in health research.

Our discussions here at Williamsburg give us new confidence in the prospects for a recovery. We have strengthened our resolve to deal cooperatively with continuing problems so as to promote a sound and sustainable recovery, bringing new jobs and a better life for the people of our own countries and of the world.

We have agreed to meet again next year and have accepted the British Prime Minister's invitation to meet in the United Kingdom.

Annex
Strengthening economic cooperation for growth and stability

I. We have examined in the light of our experience the procedures outlined in the undertakings agreed at Versailles last year which seek to ensure greater monetary stability in the interest of balanced growth and progress of the world economy.

II. We reaffirm the objectives of achieving non-inflationary growth of income and employment, and promoting exchange market stability through policies designed to bring about greater convergence of economic performance in this direction.

III. We are reinforcing our multilateral cooperation with the International Monetary Fund in its surveillance activities, according to the procedures agreed at Versailles, through the following approach:

A. We are focusing on near-term policy actions leading to convergence of economic conditions in the medium term. The overall medium-term perspective remains essential, both to ensure that short-term policy innovations do not lead to divergence and to reassure business and financial markets.

B. In accordance with the agreement reached at Versailles, we are focusing our attention on issues in the monetary and financial fields including interaction with policies in other areas. We shall take fully into account the international implications of our own policy decisions. Policies and objectives that will be kept under review include:

(1) Monetary Policy. Disciplined non-inflationary growth of monetary aggregates, and appropriate interest rates, to avoid subsequent resurgence of inflation and rebound in interest rates, thus allowing room for sustainable growth.

(2) Fiscal Policy. We will aim, preferably through discipline over government expenditures, to reduce structural budget deficits and bear in mind the consequences of fiscal policy for interest rates and growth.

(3) Exchange Rate Policy. We will improve con-

sultations, policy convergence and international cooperation to help stabilize exchange markets, bearing in mind our conclusions on the exchange market intervention study.

(4) Policies Toward Productivity and Employment. While relying on market signals as a guide to efficient economic decisions, we will take measures to improve training and mobility of our labour forces, with particular concern for the problems of youth forces, with particular concern for the problems of youth unemployment, and promote continued structural adjustment, especially by:

—Enhancing flexibility and openness of economies and financial markets.

—Encouraging research and development as well as profitability and productive investment.

—Continued efforts in each country, and improved international cooperation, where appropriate, on structural adjustment measures (e.g., regional, sectoral, energy policies).

IV. We shall continue to assess together regularly in this framework the progress we are making, consider any corrective action which may be necessary from time to time, and react promptly to significant changes.

Appendix C

Eric Kierans resigned as Federal Minister of Communications in April, 1971, citing many of the points he discusses in the Massey Lectures. Below are the texts of his resignation and Prime Minister Trudeau's reply.

Ottawa, April 28th, 1971

My dear Prime Minister:

I appreciate very much our lengthy discussion yesterday in which I expressed my concern about the economic problems, particularly employment, facing Canada in the seventies. Challenges which did not exist ten years ago now present themselves and demand a total re-examination of all elements of our economic policy. The rise of the international corporation, for example, is leading some economists and businessmen to talk in terms of gross world production as a better index of economic growth than the sum of national products. This may be, although I sense no similar concern with the distribution of that product. One can detect, however, the implicit assumption that Canada is to be assigned the role of supplier of resources presumably because we have them and also because we do not have a sufficient domestic market to justify their conversion into finished or semi-finished products here at home.

Economic policy is put together from a variety of elements, but the overriding objective of all nations in the seventies must be the attainment of full employment, however defined, as the best guarantee of political, social, and economic stability. To this end, all elements of policy—monetary, fiscal, commercial, energy and resources, agricultural, regional development—must be interconnected to ensure that they do not work at cross purposes and at the expense of overall objectives.

It is in this realm of ideas and policy that I wish to concentrate my efforts. Economic growth is not unlimited. Even with an exponential increase in capital and population—three billion now, six billion people by the year 2000—a diminishing supply of non-renewable resources will restrain world growth. Canada is fortunate in its resource base and can insist on exports with a higher labour content. Tax concessions that force the pace of our raw material exports or favour the over-employment of capital, which we have to import, at the expense of labour which is in surplus would not be consistent with long-run Canadian growth and employment objectives. If Canada is to be an industrial force in the 1980s, we must be prepared now to husband our resources and to select those areas in which we can be internationally competitive and to manage and invest in the resources, physical and human, that will give us a compelling position.

To challenge openly long-established policies and practices would be embarrassing to my colleagues and to you, and unfair, if I were to remain in the Cabinet. Therefore, I ask you to accept my resignation as Minister of Communications, effective immediately. I leave with real regret.

I fully support the national unity policies of the government and I am certain that these will achieve a better and a united Canada. In my own sphere of activity, I have greatly enjoyed the challenge that you entrusted to me as Minister of Communications.

With my warmest personal regards, I am

   Sincerely yours,

   (signed) Eric Kierans.

       Ottawa, April 29, 1971.

Dear Eric,

It was with regret that I received your request to resign as Minister of Communications and it is with reluctance that I shall recommend to the Governor General that it be accepted.

I fully share your concern about the economic future of Canada as do all your colleagues. While your own views have not always prevailed in the frequent discussions the Cabinet has had on this subject, they have nevertheless added a dimension that has helped provide the broad perspective within which our decisions have been made. It is not only I, but all of your colleagues who will miss your contribution.

As Minister of Communications, you have played a most important role in defining the problems and helping to shape Canada's course in this difficult and challenging field.

I would also like to express my thanks for all the other contributions that you have made to the government and to the people of Canada.

While you will no longer be participating in Cabinet, as a member of the Liberal Caucus your views on all matters will still command the government's attention.

I appreciate the courtesy you have shown and the spirit you have exhibited in handling the difficult personal dilemma that has faced you.

With warmest personal regards,

Yours sincerely,

(Signed) P.E. Trudeau